THE
POWER
THAT CHANGES THE
WORLD

CREATING ETERNAL IMPACT
IN THE HERE AND NOW

BILL JOHNSON

Chosen

a division of Baker Publishing Group
Minneapolis, Minnesota

Published by Chosen Books
11400 Hampshire Avenue South
Bloomington, Minnesota 55438
www.chosenbooks.com

Chosen Books is a division of
Baker Publishing Group, Grand Rapids, Michigan

Printed in the United States of America

Library of Congress Cataloging-in-Publication Data

Johnson, Bill.
    The power that changes the world : creating eternal impact in the here and now / Bill Johnson.
        pages cm
    Summary: "Become heaven's agent of change, like Joseph, Daniel, and Solomon, with these simple, practical ways to release Kingdom power in your everyday world"— Provided by publisher.
    ISBN 978-0-8007-9686-0 (pbk. : alk. paper)
    1. Christianity and culture. 2. Change—Religious aspects—Christianity. 3. Power (Christian theology) I. Title
BR115.C8J57 2015
269—dc23   2015015725

In keeping with biblical principles of creation stewardship, Baker Publishing Group advocates the responsible use of our natural resources. As a member of the Green Press Initiative, our company uses recycled paper when possible. The text paper of this book is composed in part of post-consumer waste.

Cover design by LOOK Design Studio

green press INITIATIVE

15   16   17   18   19   20   21   7   6   5   4   3   2   1

I dedicate this book to the thousands of graduates of Bethel School of Supernatural Ministry. You constantly inspire me by your sacrifice and passion. My prayer is that this book will be a strength to you as you give yourselves to help shape the course of world history and see cities and nations transformed by this wonderful Gospel of Jesus Christ.

Contents

Foreword by Jack Hayford   7
Acknowledgments   9

1. The Greenhouse Effect   11
2. God Has a Dream   23
3. The Profound Prototype   33
4. The Reformer   47
5. The Nature of the Gift   61
6. The Big Test   75
7. The Power of Beauty   97
8. What Jesus Preached   111
9. Loving Babylon   131
10. Erasing Lines   149
11. No Devil, No Problem?   165
12. A Theology of Blessing   179
13. The Power of the Broken   197
14. Living Full   207

Foreword

I wish that every pastor could (and would) experience a visit to Bethel Church in Redding, California. Without hesitation, I assure you that the likelihood that you will gain inspiration and insight is great. You will also observe integrity in the way the leadership teaches and governs amid the workings of the Holy Spirit.

This is because of what lies at the heart of the way Bill Johnson leads and teaches the congregation from the Word of God. He faithfully pursues and earnestly heeds the wisdom of God.

Although you will find some refreshing or "renewed" styles of ministry at Bethel, you will also find that the church is on a quest to avoid both the reticence of fear and the presumption of the excitable. I make this observation by reason of having ministered at Bethel and discovered that this church is not a circus, as one critic claimed. It is a pastureland where the lost or broken sheep of Christ's flock are saved and healed, and where a congregation of thousands worships and is fed on the bread, milk and meat of the Word of God. The people are taught with passion and ministered to with faith that is applied with wisdom.

The fact that I can assert the above establishes no claim for Bethel as a "perfect" church. It does assure anyone, however, that Bethel is being "perfected" effectively and faithfully by wise, caring, discerning and sensitive leaders who honor this proverb: "Wisdom is the principal thing; therefore get wisdom. And in all your getting, get understanding" (Proverbs 4:7).

I believe your encounter with this book will expose you to "principal things"—the kind of things that, wisely applied, will afford you an opportunity to gain perspective on attitudes, practices and truths that anyone would do well to gather and make into life principles.

Jack Hayford, founding pastor, The Church On The Way

Acknowledgments

I want to give special thanks to Michael Van Tinteren, Kristy Tillman, Mary Berck and Judy Franklin for your help. I cannot imagine life without you on my personal team.

1

The Greenhouse Effect

A number of years ago I was speaking at a conference in the Netherlands. During an afternoon break our host took us to see some of the beauty of his country. We saw the windmills, the waterways, the dykes and some other things that contribute to the uniqueness and wonder of this nation. Because it was November, it was also windy, cold and rainy. This made the tour unpleasant. So that we could continue our sightseeing, he took us to one of the large greenhouses that contained a portion of the country's incredible tulip crop. Holland's tulip-growing industry produces about 80 percent of the world's supply of that gorgeous flower.

Once inside, we saw row after row of beautiful flowers in every color, all planted in color-coded sections. The weather conditions in the greenhouse were completely different from the outdoors. While you would never consider it warm inside, it was pleasant. Plus, we were just glad to get in out of the

cold. As we walked through the amazing selection of flowers, we noticed a photographer taking pictures of a gorgeous
bride getting ready for her wedding. She was posing next
to a manmade pond. Her reflection on the water made for
some spectacular photos. Add to that setting the brilliant
colors of the extraordinary flowers surrounding her, and you
can imagine the beauty captured in her wedding pictures. It
was wonderful. In a sense, though, it was another reality,
because none of what we saw inside would survive outside
the walls of that greenhouse. The flowers would not survive,
and there certainly would not be a bride in her bridal gown
out in that weather.

In order to have a continuous supply of tulips available
to ship all over the world, growers needed to find a way to
grow them in inclement weather. The answer to this dilemma
was the greenhouse, a building designed to enable growers
to control temperature, light and moisture so that the plants
inside will grow easily. Just as a greenhouse is a controlled
atmosphere that enables the growth and development of spe-
cific plants, so is the nature of a Kingdom culture. It changes
what is possible in any environment. Done correctly, it is an
atmosphere impregnated with the presence of God and the
values of His Kingdom, and it influences how life is lived.

Establishing a Kingdom culture is vital because in most
cities people do not realize that the demonic realms that were
given permission to influence that city are often influencing
their thinking. What a Kingdom atmosphere does is give
people permission to think for themselves—to think clearly,
which is the essence of the freedom that only the Holy Spirit
can bring. Grace really is irresistible for those who see it
clearly. Influencing the atmosphere in a place helps set the
stage in such a way that people are much more likely to

respond to the profound invitation given in the good news of the Kingdom. This is the *greenhouse effect.*

The Cart before the Horse

Throughout history, believers have given themselves to making an impact on the world with the message of salvation. Without a doubt, salvation is the greatest miracle of all—the forgiveness of sin and the transformation of a life. It is also the greatest need of humanity. In the process of discipleship that follows, we work to instill the values God has for us in all areas of our everyday lives. Embracing and displaying these values in a godly lifestyle reveals in many ways whether we are following Jesus or just attending church.

The goal of most believers is not only to convert people to Jesus Christ, but also to influence how life is lived in their homes, and also in their cities. The impact of the Church on the value system of our cities has been strong at some times, and seemingly nonexistent at other times. We must find out why and embrace the principles that foster change and transformation in the world around us. This is part of the reason we are here.

True disciples are governed by common values. For example, every group of believers wants to see healthy family life, with children growing up to become contributors to society. We also hate the abuse we have seen of women and children, and we are desperate to see that abomination removed from society.

Another thing we greatly value is seeing businesses succeed. They influence the culture and identity of their city by giving place to the rise of genuine city fathers and mothers. There is a hunger in a Kingdom culture for success to come without the pride and arrogance that often accompany wealth. Real success enables people to serve their community more effectively, and we ache for such values to permeate our culture.

As believers, we all want to see honest politicians elected who represent us well, and more importantly, who represent a biblically mandated value system. It would be wonderful to experience an admiration for leaders again instead of feeling as though we are electing the lesser of two evils.

We long, as well, to see members of the media shaped by personal integrity and driven by a value for the truth. The bent toward prostituting the reputation of others for the sake of fame or income has to stop.

There is also a great hunger among us to see the medical community thrive with excellence, while its workers maintain the heart of a servant. It would be a dream come true if we found that this great part of every community had discovered the connection between spirit, soul and body. Part of that dream would be seeing them provide healthcare to the whole person through divine wisdom.

Many of us love entertainment, but we are tired of seeing the reprobate ideas of one person put on the screen in the name of art. God is the ultimate entertainer, causing us all to wonder at His works. He displays His phenomena for our edification, education and delight. We long for creative people to learn from the Creator and be empowered to take their necessary place in society.

This list of values is really endless as we dream of what the ultimate community and nation would look like. The solution is not for the Church to take control of these realms. Historically, it has never helped us when we fight for control, nor has it helped our influence in society. It is much better for us to accept promotion when it comes, but to focus on embracing our influence as servants.

Seeing a Kingdom culture established on earth is the dream of God, and it must become the dream of His people. Abraham, the father of faith, illustrated its importance, as he, too, longed for a city whose builder and maker is God (see Hebrews 11:10). Perhaps this is the way of faith. When Jesus brought correction to the religious leaders of His day, He told them to prove their identity through "doing the deeds of Abraham" (see John 8:39). Is it possible that Abraham's dream of that city influenced how he expressed his faith? I think so. It would be nearly impossible to separate the two.

My story of visiting the Netherlands illustrates the *greenhouse effect* on how life is lived around us. Culture is made up of the attitudes, values and priorities of a particular nation, city, social group or organization. All cultures enable the development of social norms, both good and bad. If the culture is right, it enables *the desired plants to grow easily.* (The *plants*, of course, are Kingdom values, attitudes and priorities.) The mistake that we have made is to target the goals we want to realize without giving attention to shaping culture.

In other words, we try to grow tulips in freezing weather. For example, we try to build healthy families without addressing the atmosphere in our community that enables that "plant" to grow easily. It is not either/or. It is both/and. Should we be successful in shaping culture, you can imagine what it would look like to see the right "plants" grow easily. Successfully shaping culture makes healthy families the norm. When we try to influence family values, however, we are viewed as people with an agenda, people who use religion as the basis to take over a society to accomplish their own goals. But society views servants completely differently. When we are seen as servants who have no agenda except to love, we are given access to the heart of the community.

Giving Who We Are

I doubt there are very many believers who would not want to influence the culture around them. Unfortunately, we know too little of the culture of heaven to be trusted with such an assignment here and now. For this reason, we have been commanded to seek first His Kingdom. His world provides the template for our life and ministry here on earth. *First* means it is the top priority, and it enables us to have a greater impact on the world around us. Heaven is the model God set for us by which we are to approach life. Much of what people experience in church life is *Christian culture*, but not necessarily Kingdom culture. I will explain more of that later in this book, but for now, suffice to say that some things work in our little piece of the world that have no chance of working outside our Christian circles. That is part of the reason we must pursue the Kingdom first and foremost. True Kingdom experiences and values are transferable to every part of society.

If you doubt that, consider this: If everyone were born again in our cities, it would be wonderful. But that in itself would not solve our cities' problems. Look at any church in your city for evidence of that reality. Our churches are filled with unresolved issues, all of which pertain to how well we do the "Kingdom lifestyle." The problems would only increase because we think being saved gives us the right to tell people how to live. Yet if the average church board were put in charge of a major corporation, it would go bankrupt in a short period of time. I honestly don't say that to be cruel. Some systems work in a religious environment that would not last a week in any other. But those who discover the ways of the Kingdom can have influence in any environment—simply because Kingdom ways work anywhere.

Without the values of heaven defining who we are and how we live, we are not in a position to influence the world's culture. If the Kingdom of God does not influence how we conduct our lives within the Church, we can never expect God to empower us to influence the cultures of the world around us. We can only give away what we have received. We receive by experience.

A Primary Stumbling Block

Many believers treat with disdain this assignment of shaping culture, because they feel that sin and darkness must increase for Jesus to return. When sin increases, a perverted sense of encouragement often arises in the hearts of many Christians because it is a sign of the end, and of course we all want to go to heaven. Their thought is that cultural transformation with Kingdom-oriented values is supposed to happen in the Millennium or in heaven, but it is not for now. Such foolishness has kept us from the place of impact. Our thoughts become more shaped by the presence of evil around us than by the promise of God within us. Either we make an impact on the world around us, or it makes an impact on us.

The apostle Paul revealed a profound secret when he stated, "to the intent that now the manifold wisdom of God might be made known by the church to the principalities and powers in the heavenly places" (Ephesians 3:10). We believers are to put culturally transforming wisdom on display *now*. God's wisdom affects first the person who has it, then everyone under his or her influence. But the intended impact is not complete until the spirit realm in heavenly places recognizes that God's wisdom is working in us! Even angels can learn from our example of divine wisdom because they have never seen it displayed through redeemed humanity working together as one Body.

We often draw unhealthy conclusions about how things are supposed to end. When we do that, we let our assumptions shape how we see our place in this world. Our opinion of the last days must never undermine our commission. Jesus commanded us to pray for life on earth to be as it is in heaven. That happens through His Kingdom becoming manifest—when the King has dominion over the everyday affairs of life. He commanded us to take the good news of this Kingdom to every people group in the world. Whenever we have a conviction about the last days that wrongly affects our commitment and hope for fulfilling our assignment, then we have given that conviction the wrong place in our hearts. My intent is not to tell you what to believe about the end times. My desire is to help you understand your assignment as it corresponds to God's dreams.

We can easily become ineffective through our lack of clear prophetic vision. And that was the subject spoken of in the famous verse, "Where there is no vision, the people perish" (Proverbs 29:18 KJV). The Amplified Bible calls this vision the "redemptive revelation of God." My favorite rendition comes from The Passion Translation: "When there is no clear prophetic vision, people quickly wander astray." Prophetic vision is always deeply rooted in hope. That is the purpose of vision. As someone once said, vision gives pain a purpose.

Without hope, we don't have the endurance needed to see His dreams realized.

The Power of Number Two

Joseph, Daniel and Esther all influenced nations. But none of them was an elected official or held any position of rulership over a nation. Yet the culture and well-being of several nations were in their range of influence. Their secret was to serve their assigned leader as unto the Lord. They each took their role seriously even though they could have listed many legitimate reasons to abandon their post, not the least of which was that the leaders they served were devil worshipers.

Whenever we think that the environment we live in is too dark for us to display the Gospel correctly, these three testify against us. They did not even have access to the same realm of anointing and baptism in the Spirit that is available to us, yet they all succeeded. We, then, are without excuse.

When we reduce our influence to elections and popular vote, we disgrace the One who covenanted with us never to leave us or forsake us. That political spirit is the leaven Jesus warned us of in Mark 8 when He said to be careful of the leaven of Herod. The political system is real, but it is seriously inferior to the Kingdom of God. The covenant of His abiding presence makes it possible for us to live with great transformational influence. The presence of God is the supreme value of His world, and it must affect ours.

Many think our role is to be in charge of businesses, political parties, schools and the like. I am happy when believers are given those kinds of promotions. But the thought that this is the only way for us to bring influence is not only

19

an error; it disqualifies the majority in the Body of Christ from having genuine impact on their world. So we must ask ourselves how we want to affect the world around us. It comes down to this: Do we want ownership or influence? What we have the capacity to rule in ownership is much smaller than what we have the ability to influence. And since the Kingdom of God (within us) is like leaven, I believe He wants us to prioritize permeating the world around us until we bring Kingdom influence into every realm of society. Influence is supreme. It is the testimony of Joseph, Daniel and Esther that shouts what might be possible in our lifetime.

History Speaks

History testifies against those without this hope for transformation, as the transformation of cities and nations has been done before. It happened in both the Old and New Testaments. We must give ourselves to "keep the testimony" (see Deuteronomy 6:17) of transformation and position ourselves for the same in our lifetime.

Careful study shows us it is possible for the values of heaven to affect how life is lived here on earth. All that is needed is a group of people who will lay everything on the line to believe for God's best in their generation as they explore the nature of His world. It is the testimony of the Great Awakenings. In reality, the supernatural breakthroughs of the past are putting a demand on us to believe for the same in our day. The history of divine intervention is summoning us into the future. This is our destiny and call. It is another paradox of the Kingdom to see the past pull us into our future. Only God's history can do that.

On July 17, 1859, Charles Spurgeon, one of the greatest preachers of all time, brought a message entitled "The Story of God's Mighty Acts." In this sermon he declared how the miracles of divine intervention in the past have the power to shape the present. Listen to his cry (emphasis added):

> When people hear about what God used to do, one of the things they say is: "Oh, that was a very long while ago." . . . I thought it was God that did it. Has God changed? Is he not an immutable God, the same yesterday, today and forever? Does not that furnish an argument to prove that what God has done at one time he can do at another? Nay, I think I may push it a little further and say *what he has done once is a prophecy of what he intends to do again. . . . Whatever God has done . . . is to be looked upon as a precedent. . . .* [Let us] with earnestness seek that God would restore to us the faith of the men of old, that we may richly enjoy his grace as in the days of old.[1]

It is irresponsible to position ourselves for the return of Christ at the expense of bringing about the transformation He commanded of us. His return is certain and will be glorious! But it is not my job to go to heaven. Only He can get me there. My assignment is to bring heaven to earth through my prayers and acts of radical obedience. To ignore my assignment is to fail in helping create the atmosphere that makes it possible for the *right plants* to grow—the plants that are the actual evidences of the reformation we long for, that are tangible expressions of *the kindness of God that leads to repentance.*

1. Charles Spurgeon, "The Story of God's Mighty Acts," The Spurgeon Archive, http://www.spurgeon.org/sermons/0263.htm.

Architects of Culture

We are architects of culture. We make daily decisions that either contribute to a culture shaped by values of the Kingdom of God or that undermine such a culture. We must live to affect the thoughts, values and purposes of the world around us. People with a clear vision are much more likely to influence these realms as they live with intention. Many of those around us come to their own conclusions about these things in the absence of a clear voice. Such misdirected values are the product of disappointment, fatherlessness and sin. But there is a better way. It is possible to be an intentional voice, illustrating the wonders of the Kingdom of God. The need of the hour is a voice, followed by an example. We model these values in our relationships, both with those who are for us and those who are against us. When honor is displayed in both situations, we gain the right to speak. And speak we must, in order for the mystery of the power of preaching to be realized.

We illustrate values with how we steward our God-given moments in life. Values that are driven by love and hope are easy for a city to fully embrace. This is our God-given mandate.

2

God Has a Dream

If we are to be involved in God's purposes on the earth, it would help us to have an idea of what His will might be. Too often, our definitions of His will have little practical application. My dear friend and associate, Kris Vallotton, uses a brilliant analogy to illustrate this point. Let's say you have a 1955 Chevy you want restored to its former beauty. And in this story, let's say I own a restoration shop known for its excellence. When you bring your car to me, you tell me to spare no expense to make the car as beautiful as possible.

Let's say about halfway through the project, I discover that you plan to enter your car in a demolition derby where the cars crash into each other until all of them are destroyed except the last one left running. Do you think that knowledge will affect the quality of my work?

You know it will. The intended outcome of something has everything in the world to do with our vision and hope for it, and with the quality of labor we put into it. And much of the Church has a demolition derby kind of approach to the last days. They believe the Church will be filled with sin and many will fall away, barely escaping the judgment to come. It is no wonder so few believers live with hope.

The Church of the last hundred years or so has labored under the idea that our only hope is to be rescued from the powers of darkness. Our faith is no longer in the power of the Gospel. But as Georgian Banov, a great musician and minister of the Gospel from Eastern Europe, has said, "If you can't be free from sin until you die, then Jesus isn't your Savior, death is."

Devastation looms everywhere, and for many, the only answer is to go to heaven. While that may seem discerning and spiritual to some, it reveals our lack of faith in God's promises and our weak understanding of the power of the blood of Jesus. His glorious redemptive work made it possible for us to see God's purposes accomplished for humanity while we are on earth. The escapism approach completely undermines the significance of the message we carry that *the Kingdom is at hand.*

Neither the Reformation nor the two Great Awakenings came from the kind of thinking that says we need to be rescued. We are designed as overcomers. Those who are convinced of the heart of God for people carry a conviction of the superiority of *His* message. The Gospel is good news for eternity, but also for now. It must be used to confront the inferior ideals of darkness that masquerade as intelligence every time the question arises, "Where is your God?" (see Psalm 42:9–11; Joel 2:15–19). Ideals "raised up against the knowledge of God" are mere illusions of grandeur working to distract us from the promises that God has given us for the here and now (2 Corinthians 10:5 NASB). And we must confront them through infectious confidence in God and through the courage to embrace His purposes. Hope always speaks the loudest.

Oftentimes we take the great promises of Scripture and put them off into a period of time for which we have no responsibility—the Millennium or eternity in heaven. One of the ultimate expressions of arrogance is to think that we know ahead of time what is about to happen, and to let that cause us to become ineffective in our assigned purpose and call. When did the disciples know and understand ahead of time what God was going to do? I cannot find one instance. Jesus prophesied to them, but they only understood what He meant *after* it happened. What if we took a cue from their example and kept our lives firmly anchored in our commission, without adjusting it to accommodate our unbelief? I believe true Kingdom success would be the result.

At the very minimum, we must bring Scripture's extraordinary promises to God and ask if it might be possible for Him to fulfill them in our lifetime. Because we are *believers*, we must look to the possibility contained in a promise more than we look to the effect of the evil that surrounds us. This is the responsibility of the *faith-full*. On top of that, we are to prophesy according to our faith (see Romans 12:6). We should consider what it looks like to declare the word of the Lord when it is backed by faith in the purposes and plans of God. It has to look different from the typical word that requires no faith to see it fulfilled.

What Did We Lose?

Jesus said He came to save that which was lost (see Matthew 18:11). Certainly people separated from God because of sin are considered *lost*. For this reason, we pursue bringing the message of salvation to every person. But is that the full reach of the statement Jesus made? I think not. He did not come to do a partial job. His redemptive work was complete, reaching far beyond our understanding. People are saved. But then so are cities, nations, tribes and tongues. In one commission, He commanded us to preach the Gospel of the Kingdom to all creation. That was not a typo. God wants everything restored, because the blood of Jesus was enough to cover the whole cause and effect of sin on all of creation. Perhaps that is part of what Paul meant in Romans 8:19–22, when he addressed the impact of the message on all that God had made.

God planted humanity on a planet where darkness resided because of the expulsion of Satan from heaven. The devil was removed from his place of authority when he longed to be worshiped alongside God. He was removed from his responsibilities among the three archangels—Gabriel, Michael and Lucifer (as he was called)—and he lost his place in heaven and ended up occupying planet earth. He also brought with him a third of the angels, who were no doubt under his charge while in heaven.

The dominion God gave to humankind in the Genesis 1:28–29 commission was designed to bring destruction to the powers of darkness through God's delegated authority. We are the only part of all creation made in the image of God. Instead of God destroying the powers of darkness, He assigned the task to those He created in His image. But when we obeyed the devil instead of God, we gave our authority to the powers of darkness and became slaves of the one we obeyed. Since a master owns a slave and all his or her possessions, in the fall we lost the dominion God had given us.

That is part of the discussion the devil had with Jesus during the temptation in Luke 4, when he said, "I will give you all this domain and its glory; for *it has been handed over to me*, and I give it to whomever I wish" (verse 6 NASB, emphasis added). The devil offered this to Jesus if He would only bow in worship. Of course, Jesus said no and took it all back through His violent death on the cross and the resurrection that followed. Once again, this reveals the wisdom of God.

The dominion we lost is one of the things Jesus came to take back. He bought us through shedding His blood as the sacrificial lamb when He took our place in death. He then rose from the dead and announced that He had taken the keys back and now had all authority in heaven and on earth. *All* has to include that which we forfeited when we obeyed the serpent instead of God. Jesus then called us to the *restored purpose* found in His commission—to preach the Gospel of the Kingdom, and in the process, disciple nations. This is, in effect, a return to plan A, which is the expression of His dominion through His delegated authority. This is the authority He originally gave to Adam and Eve in the Garden when He said, "Be fruitful and multiply, and fill the earth, and subdue it" (Genesis 1:28 NASB).[2]

The word *subdue* is a word that implies conflict and a process that needs to take place owing to the opposition that already existed here on earth. It is a military-type term revealing that we were born into a war—God created us as people of solution and purpose. Such realities of conflicts and solutions remain today for those who will adjust their thinking to the possibilities that exist through the profound

2. A much more complete discussion of this subject is found in chapter 2 of my book *When Heaven Invades Earth: A Practical Guide to a Life of Miracles* (Destiny Image, 2013).

nature and power of our message. Think of it—we were designed for problems. His purpose and plan is complete, lacking in nothing and ready to be administered to any and every ailment of mankind. And that includes the ailments found in governments.

Much of our Christian culture has evolved in the absence of the ultimate values and purposes that God has for the planet. We also have a tendency to forget what has been accomplished before our time, which is supposed to give us courage for our day. Instead, we look at things like the Reformation as oddities that were necessary to prepare us for the end, not things that we are to build on or take to the next level. The generations of believers who helped bring about the two Great Awakenings and the Reformation did not sit back and think, *It's time to get a few souls saved, and then let's get rescued from the forces of evil.* Instead, they believed in the ability of God to accomplish His desires through a yielded people. They looked beyond the evil of their day and saw the heart of God revealed in His promises, which deal with every malady humanity has ever experienced.

God has the answer. Yes, it is Jesus. His redemptive work made possible the restoration of the planet, its people and His purposes. The practical application of what Jesus made possible is the answer to the hellish conditions that afflict people's lives. According to the Great Commission, our message is incomplete without preaching the Kingdom of God. This Kingdom has a King, and He is *at hand*. That means the King and His Kingdom are *now*, and are within reach.

The very fact that *bad news sells* reveals the appetite that exists in the world around us, and tragically even within the Church. Instead of shaping culture around us, we are all too often shaped by it. If you want to write a bestseller, write about the collapse of a nation or the economy, or write about the destruction of a people group by God's judgment. And what sells even better are the books about evil taking over society and plunging us into ultimate destruction until the Antichrist takes over.

I would never suggest that God is not the Judge or that there is not a Day of Judgment coming. It is just that our appetite for bad news actually insulates us from realizing the devastating effects of our unbelief. Evil often thrives in the absence of an authentic righteous standard. Blind to our unbelief, we become convinced of the devastating power of evil over the surpassing richness of God's grace. Unbelief then sculpts our last-days theology. The sad reality is that all the evil that has happened in this generation has happened on our watch. And none of it was the will or intention of God. Evil is not necessary.

God identifies sin, error and the destructive effects of a lifestyle of evil. There are consequences to a society giving itself over to evil. For me to suggest otherwise would be misleading. It is just that all too often, I hear the bad news without hearing the Church ever speak of the antidote. God has a practical and doable answer for every problem. When He drafted His plan for the earth, He took our sin, weakness and ignorance into account. They do not intimidate Him. This is the hour when the grace of God is abundantly present in the darkest places. All that is needed are willing vessels—ones who will boldly proclaim the Kingdom at hand and then demonstrate its reality. Perhaps this is why Jesus said He did not pray for the world. Rather, He instructed His disciples to pray for laborers. The world is ready to hear a message they could both live and die for, if the authentic can be put on display.

How God Sees

We tend to think the Gospel is only for us as individuals. Not seeing the full reach of His redemptive touch often weakens our understanding. The Gospel must include cities and nations as we pray and plan. Scripture frequently shows us God's heart for the big picture. The mercy He showed in Jonah's day was for the *great city* (God's definition) of Nineveh. He often directed His messages through the prophets to cities and nations. The letters of Christ to the churches in Revelation 2 and 3 were actually addressed to the angel of an entire city. In the gospels, Jesus brought a rebuke to the three cities He ministered in the most—Chorazin, Bethsaida and Capernaum—because they did not repent after seeing His display of the Kingdom.

The point is, God thinks in terms of people groups and not just individuals. Even the salvation that came through Jesus' blood was intended to come to entire families: "You will be saved, you and all your household" (Acts 11:14 NASB). And while no one is grandfathered into salvation (in other words, being saved apart from their own faith), God sees a bigger picture than just salvation for individuals.

Setting our hearts on what He has set His heart on is extremely liberating and empowering. We often make the mistake of reducing His impact on us to a survival mentality, instead of becoming the victors He made us to be. Perhaps this is what the writer of Psalm 78:41, 56 addressed when he said that God's people had tempted Him by limiting Him. How did they limit Him? They forgot that He is the God who invades the impossible. They forgot His miracle testimonies.

In other words, God is the solver of impossible problems. He often does this through the co-laboring effect of His people.

Our Faith Works

Can people truly be free from both the lifestyle and effects of sin in their lives? Unquestionably, yes. If one person can be free, then certainly a whole family can find freedom. If a whole family can live in the liberty that Jesus purchased for them, then the extended family can enjoy this gift as well.

What about that family's neighborhood? We have seen it happen. One household after another tastes of the goodness of God, until an entire neighborhood becomes engulfed in the purposes of God. Such transformation is in the heart of God. And if it can happen in one neighborhood, then certainly it can spread, until a whole city is under the influence of this wonderful grace of God.

Divine reasoning says if it can happen to one city, then it can happen to a second city and a third, and beyond. It is then possible for this domino effect to take place until a whole nation comes under the influence of the reign of a perfect Father. It is needed, it is possible and it is *at hand*.

Is it possible for a business to operate by Kingdom principles and step into a place of economic healing and prosperity, until its owners become a blessing to their entire community? Of course it is possible. This has happened countless times. If God can heal the economy of one business, He can do it for two or three, or more. What God does for one is the testimony of what He would like to do for all. The financial healing in one business prophesies God's intention to heal the economy of a city or nation. This is the heart of God—big, powerful and ready to accomplish His purposes in our day. And we must change our thinking until it includes the big picture.

The oak tree is in the acorn. Much of what we consider impossible or out of reach already exists in the smaller breakthroughs we have already experienced. That seed of answered prayer carries the DNA of heaven to see God's purposes accomplished here on earth. The prophet Elijah ran for cover from the coming rain when he saw a cloud the size of a man's hand (see 1 Kings 18:44). He knew the potential of the moment because it was a God moment. Approaching life from the promises of God positions us for breakthroughs that others consider unreasonable. We were born to live a life in which the unreasonable yields to the power of the name of Jesus spoken through our lips.

Jesus said it: The Kingdom is at hand. Now we get to unravel the mysteries of His world, heaven, knowing that it was His pleasure to give them to us as an inheritance (see Matthew 13:11). It is through His gift of wisdom and understanding that we have the honor of living intentionally toward the darkest places of our world and presenting the solutions found in the reality of His world. Let it be on earth as it is in heaven!

3

The Profound Prototype

I remember a conversation I had with a friend when I was about twelve years old. I asked him what he would choose if he could have anything he wanted. His answer was typical for any twelve-year-old, although I don't remember what it was now. My answer was not typical for a twelve-year-old, nor was it normal for me. I told him I wanted wisdom.

It might sound as though I were a very spiritual child whose values were intact at an early age. That is not even close to the truth. I just remembered from Sunday school that God gave this "one wish" opportunity to a king named Solomon, and it seemed to work out pretty well for him. It looked like a good choice to me, although I could not have explained what wisdom was if my life depended on it.

It is interesting how God takes what we think are insignificant confessions and prayers and uses them to shape our lives. I love and believe in radical, life-changing encounters with Him. I have had them myself and have even studied the effects of such encounters on other people's lives. I recently wrote a whole book called *Defining Moments* (Whitaker House, forthcoming) about such encounters. They are amazing. Unlike those moments, the moment I had with my friend seemed anything but spectacular. Yet somehow that moment has shaped my life. Wisdom remains my quest to this day.

In the time since that defining moment in my life, I have realized that it was Solomon who provided us with the most unusual prototype for life on this planet.

Practical Pursuits

About fifteen years ago, my attention began to turn to *culture* and how it is shaped in a city, state and country. During that season, I visited a city in the United States that was known as the headquarters of a particular cult. It was interesting to see how much that religious group shaped the culture of their environment, even though most of the people who lived there did not believe what this group taught. Outwardly, most of the citizens did not belong to the group. Inwardly, they thought like the group and held similar values. I noticed both in that city and in other places around the world that we are either at odds with a prevailing evil culture or we are influenced by it. There is no middle ground.

Think about the example of that city—if a group that promotes lies can shape culture so effectively, how much more is shaping culture a viable pursuit for those who embrace and declare truth? Truth bears fruit that everyone longs for. Jesus told us that "wisdom is vindicated by all her children" (Luke 7:35 NASB), meaning that true wisdom is proven by the fruitfulness of its influence and values. As His disciples, our goal should be to impact how people think, what they value and ultimately how we all live as citizens of our communities. We will not accomplish this through religious coercion. We will do it by serving others well and by illustrating that His ways are best. The wise are called to shape the value systems of the people they serve.

Our staff at Bethel Church began to seek wisdom and understanding about how to become the catalyst for change in our city. Much of our study, prayer and discussion centered on this theme. As happens often, many of my friends and associates started studying this subject at the same time as I did, independent of my direction. It became apparent that this was a theme directed by the Holy Spirit, as we were each surprised at the similarity of teachings that came from different members of our team. Surprised . . . but yet not. We had witnessed the influence of our sovereign God in this manner before. It seems to serve as a good indicator that we are on the right course when we find ourselves saying the same things at the same time without prior discussion between us.

Our target slowly changed from simply serving the local church to serving our city in ways that would benefit it, independent of the growth of the church. Actually, there was never a time when we did not want to touch our city. It has always been a priority. But this time, it was different. We wanted people touched by God where they were instead of having to come to our church to benefit from what we have to offer.

It is not that we don't want people to attend our fellowship of believers. Certainly, we are delighted when they do. We just changed the way we measure our success as a church. Our measure changed from increased attendance on Sunday to the transformed attitude and value system of our city. In biblical terms, such a measure would demonstrate the reality of heaven affecting earth as we influenced how people think and live in their homes, occupations, businesses and places of recreation. *Kingdom culture* works outside our congregational services quite well, and it is essentially what everyone longs for.

The Disciples' Prayer

Jesus never commanded anything that was not intensely practical and doable. He was not a guy who told His disciples to dig a hole and then fill it back up just to keep them busy. Busyness is an enemy of true Kingdom experience. Everything He tells us to do has redemptive influence here and now, but also ultimately has impact on eternity.

The only subject I can find the disciples asking Jesus to teach them about is prayer. The most famous prayer of all time is without question the one most often called the Lord's Prayer, found in Matthew 6. Technically it should be called the *disciples' prayer*, because it contains a confession of sin, and Jesus didn't have any sin. He was teaching the prayer to the disciples for their sake, not His.

While the entire Lord's Prayer is a profound example of the things that should concern us when we come before the Father, one phrase in particular illustrates what I am saying in this chapter: "on earth as it is in heaven." Heaven is the model for earth. In order for "on earth as it is in heaven" to become a reality, it must be practical and doable.

That one request of the disciples makes this an *apostolic prayer. Apostle* is a term that much of the Church rejects since many don't believe the office still exists today. There are some, however, for whom *apostle* has become a title worth pursuing, especially for those longing to climb the "corporate ladder" within the Church. It makes people feel powerful and significant in God to have such recognition. In the Bible, however, the apostle is the least of all, not the top of a spiritual pyramid.

It is not necessary to believe in apostles for today, though, to learn from this prayer. Consider what the term *apostle* meant in Jesus' day. Jesus borrowed the word from the Romans, who borrowed it from the Greeks. Jesus was practical, and it was this word that best described what He was building in His Church on earth—an apostolic movement. In Roman terms, the word described the lead ship in an armada of ships. The responsibility of the great company of people aboard the ship was to re-create Roman culture in a newly conquered land. They did this by introducing Rome's educational system, language, arts, road-building skills and countless other cultural features and values that had worked so well in Rome. The intention of the apostolic team sent forth by Rome was to create in the new land something so similar to Rome that if the emperor were to visit, he would feel as much at home there as he did in Rome itself.

This helps us understand the purpose of the prayer Jesus taught us much more clearly. When He said "on earth as it is in heaven," He actually meant what He said. He was not trying to keep us busy with spiritual activities until the day He comes back to rescue us from the prevailing darkness. He longs for places on the earth that remind Him of heaven, places in which He feels at home. Prayer and radical obedience make such places possible.

This is the backbone of our commission. Everything we do, from raising healthy families to preaching the Gospel, from praying for the sick to leading people to Christ, is all done to complete this glorious assignment: Pray and obey until this world looks, thinks and acts like His world.

The Hidden Keys

About ten years ago, I felt unusually impressed to look to the life of Solomon for insight into cultural transformation. I realized it would be key for me to focus on his writings and experiences. In those I would find the secrets, or hidden keys, to the transformation of cities and nations.

While I could have listed several obvious things in Solomon's life that would help me understand the subject, I did not have enough questions to ask to learn all that the Lord wanted to show me. It is hard to recognize the answers if you don't know the questions. And so began my journey to figure out what I needed to know about cultural transformation and what Solomon could teach me. This last decade then turned into a great season of experimentation with the things I discovered in Scripture. That is the best way to learn. By the way, one of the things I learned is that true Kingdom insights will work in any nation or culture around the world. The way they are expressed, however, will vary from location to location.

This new direction toward cultural transformation also required a change of heart if I was to benefit from Solomon's life. I have held contempt for his idolatry for as long as I can remember. That has not changed. But seeing his errors blinded me from seeing his successes. It was time for me to learn to *eat the meat and throw out the bones* at a whole new level, because it became evident that God had once again hidden His secrets in places I would not normally look.

Sometimes the things we want the most are hidden in the shadows of the things we most despise. This reality keeps the overcautious from finding the greater treasures of God, reaffirming the fact that we are to seek Him with *all our heart*, even when He hides Himself in darkness (see Psalm 18:11). *All* here implies that we must do our seeking in the context of total and complete abandonment to obedience. Our obedience is often measured by our willingness to go against our own biases, no matter how spiritual they seem. I am told it took Israel three hundred years to recover from Solomon's idolatry. I saw nothing good in that. Yet in the same way that honey was found in the carcass of a lion (see Judges 14:8), I found that the treasure of transformation could be found in the life of Solomon, the one who brought defilement to the entire nation of God's people.

Help, I'm a Pastor

For as long as I can remember, the highest value I held as a believer was to see the people of God built up and encouraged. I love the local church! That is the value the wonderful home I grew up in exposed me to the most. My mom and dad were pastors. They truly loved people, and they sacrificed greatly to see lives forever impacted. Their heart was to serve others and enable them to become all that God intended. I learned so much from my parents' example.

I grew up realizing that *church* was not a building, a denomination or a Sunday meeting. It was people. With that in mind, I embraced what I considered the highest call for my life—to serve the local church. At the same time, I watched as a change came into our environment. It became more and more clear to us that every believer is called as a priest unto the Lord. Our immediate discovery of this truth was first applied to our expression of worship. It was our call and honor to minister to Him with thanksgiving, praise and worship. This we did with great joy.

But as the Lord began to unravel what He meant when He called all of us priests, we discovered that this great truth also applied to our roles outside our corporate gatherings— in other words, outside the local church. The weightiness of this discovery was much like the *time-release capsules* found in medicine. Only this time, the truth of every believer being a minister to God would take decades to unpack. We have a lot to unlearn so that we can fully discover the insights we need about how to approach life outside of church activities. Priests had a dual role in ministry—to God, but also to people. Even now, it feels as if we are just beginning to understand His purposes and plans in this area.

God calls every person to be a priest (minister), but only a few will stand in pulpits. Unfortunately, pulpit ministry has long been seen as the measure of true devotion to Christ, or worse yet, it has been seen as the measure of spiritual maturity. My present ambition in saying that would never be to lessen the value we place on the missionary, the evangelist, the pastor, etc. Instead, I hope to raise the value we place on the call of God, in whatever way that call manifests in someone's life. The dentist, the lawyer, the housewife, the mechanic and all the rest are called by God to do what they do to more fully express who He is in a functioning and healthy society. To illustrate this as the Church, we are called *members of a body*. This concept also works well to illustrate how a city functions. Each person is to play a unique and necessary role in completing the whole purpose and plan of God for the people living in that community.

While I still prioritize the local church, my heart is turning more and more to our city. I realize that true success is not measured in the number of people who attend church on a Sunday, as good a thing as that may seem. Success in God's eyes is seen in the impact the message of the Kingdom has on how people think and live in my city, region and nation. In a very real sense, it is seen in *how at home God would feel in coming to our city to live.* And while that may seem impractical to some, it has become intensely practical to me. "On earth as it is in heaven" is the mandate of the Church.

Mountains of Influence

One of the metaphors that has taken center stage in the churches I work with in recent years is something called *the seven mountains of influence.* This metaphor describes different realms of society that influence the minds and values of the people within those realms. Obviously, if these segments of society do not have Kingdom values, their influence is destructive in nature. Each of these areas therefore greatly needs the influence of people who hold the values of the Kingdom.

Movements such as revivals and renewals usually start at a grassroots level with the poor in Spirit, the broken and the desperate. Imagine a fire that burns from the bottom of a wall to the top. This illustrates the nature of the movements of God. But culture is shaped from the top down. When a grassroots movement does not *burn all the way up* to the upper echelons of society (where the actual mind molders are), then the reality is that the movement is kept in its place and is largely ineffective in reaching its potential. Or, as forest officials would say, it is a *controlled burn*.

The seed of reformation is aborted when it fails to touch those who shape culture from the top down. Conversely, when we do succeed in this endeavor, the thoughts and values of the elite are influenced and shaped by the success of the broken and poor in spirit who have been changed by the power of God. And they, in turn, affect the values and thoughts of an entire society. Our role in truly shaping culture is usually dependent on our success in this mission.

These *seven mountains of influence* are realms of society that are present-day mission fields. They welcome people of excellence who come and serve. Each realm longs to see His Kingdom come, whether the head influencers (mind molders) are aware of it or not. The bottom line is that everyone wants a king like Jesus—that is why He is called the Desire of the Nations (see Haggai 2:7).

Each mountain of influence then becomes a perfect target where heaven's blueprint can be fully manifested and expressed. This emphasis on the mountains of influence in society has further strengthened our commitment to see every believer as a minister in the fullest sense of the word. With that in mind, each realm is a place where we long to see the nature of heaven realized in practical terms. It has put teeth to our commission "on earth as it is in heaven."

For us to see transformation in our cities, states and nations, the influence of the Kingdom of God must be present in all realms of society. That does not mean that believers have to be in charge of these realms. Joseph saved two nations, and he was the leader of neither. He served Pharaoh.

We underestimate the role of being number two. Since the Kingdom of God is likened unto leaven in Scripture, people who live Kingdom lifestyles simply need to be placed into these environments to have influence.

Several years ago we put this concept on a prayer card to enable our church family to pray more effectively for the transformation of our city and region. Our list is slightly different from the lists some others have published under this theme—not because it is better, but because it more accurately describes how we as a body think and function.

The Seven Mountains or Spheres of Influence

Family

We pray and serve in this realm so that covenant relationships and personal identity would be established on Kingdom principles. These are the key building blocks of society. Parenting styles, singleness, orphan care, gender issues, marriage, sexuality, divorce and aging are all to come under the influence of the mind of Christ. These areas offer great opportunities to illustrate how the Kingdom functions.

Religion

We pray and serve in this realm so that our faith and practice is anchored in what is ultimately true. Among the many voices on this mountain, the Church declares who God is and what Jesus has done to redeem all of creation. Hope has become a central theme, as those with the greatest hope will have the greatest influence. This realm must give itself for the well-being of our communities, and not feed off them for numerical success.

Economy

We pray and serve so that the system that produces, distributes and consumes wealth does so with the values of heaven in mind. Kingdom success is extremely gratifying because it is measured in impact, not just income and possessions. Business, finance, management, social justice, capitalism, socialism, prosperity, poverty and the like are all issues that involve big problems and practical solutions for those who are citizens of heaven. God's Kingdom has an effect here and now, and it must be tapped if this realm is to be put back in order.

Education

We pray and serve so that the ones called to this realm of influence would be firmly anchored in the values of heaven. The absolutes of God's world will stand the test of intellectual curiosity, defining the "who, what, when, where, why and how" we teach the next generation. Public and private schools, textbooks, literacy, indoctrination versus education, universities—all these are open targets for the ministers called to serve in this mission field. We serve a generation that longs to be empowered, that they may become what they were born to become.

Government

We pray and serve so that the system by which we rule and are ruled, along with those who rule, would represent the values of the Kingdom of God in every way. Politics, laws, the courts, taxes, prisons, the military, bureaucracies, civic duty, patriotism and activism are among the realms we must embrace if we are to fully illustrate the wonderful ideas

God has for how society should be governed. Government exists to protect its citizens—and then in that atmosphere of protection to enable the citizens to become what they were designed to become. Governments are never to prosper at the expense of their citizens; they are to prosper when their people prosper.

Arts and Media

We pray and serve so that our creative ideas, stories, music, games and talents accurately reveal the creative nature of God. Entertainment, the press, sports, novels, myths, the Internet, television and music are all wonderful gifts to society when they strengthen, encourage and give hope and refreshment to the people or open our understanding of the heart of God on a matter. These realms are primary targets of the powers of darkness because they are the best tools for communication. For this reason, God has been giving His people greater courage to love and serve well in these areas of influence.

Science and Technology

We pray and serve so our knowledge of creation and the Creator, design and the Designer, becomes more clearly manifested in how we live. Thus, we can embrace a more complete understanding of why we are alive. When we remove the concept of the Creator, we remove the idea of design. When we lose the concept of design, we lose the idea of purpose. When we lose the idea of purpose, we have destroyed the platform of destiny. When our sense of destiny is gone, we no longer have an awareness of accountability. And giving an account of our lives before God is central to who we are and why we are here. Health, medicine, innovation, sanitation, the printing press, computers, weaponry and the like are all gifts to humanity when used in a redemptive way. Learning how God views these realms is key if we are to use them well to serve the purpose of humanity on earth.

It Is Time to Reign

In his Passion Translation, Brian Simmons captured this theme brilliantly in his work on Proverbs:

> Can't you hear the voice of Wisdom? From the top of the *mountains of influence* she speaks into the gateways of the glorious city. At the place where pathways merge, at the entrance of every portal, there she stands, ready to impart understanding, shouting aloud to all who enter, preaching her sermon to those who will listen. "I'm calling to you, sons of Adam, yes, and to your daughters as well. Listen to me and you will be prudent and wise. For even the foolish and feeble can receive an understanding heart that will change their inner being. The meaning of my words will release within you revelation for you to *reign in life*. My lyrics will empower you to live by what is right."
>
> Proverbs 8:1–6, emphasis added

Like Esther of old, we were born for such a time as this. This is to be our brightest hour, if only we learn what God's world is like and embrace the privilege to serve in our world. From there it is simple implementation. With heaven as our model, we are designed to invade and fix problems here on earth as part of our *every believer is a minister* mandate. And wisdom is the key if we are to fully manifest the purposes of God on earth in our lifetime.

4

The Reformer

Imagine a city that is filled with a tangible peace—a thick, impressive atmosphere of peace that enables people to think for themselves, dream and celebrate life. Imagine a place where hope is real and measurable, so the prevailing attitude is that anything is possible. Imagine a city where prosperity touches every citizen, and there is no lack of any kind. Imagine a place where not only is there no lack, but there is creativity, beauty and stunning design everywhere you look. Prosperity takes on purpose as God's nature is seen in the things people have made. Imagine having a government that made you proud to be a citizen. Can you imagine what it would be like to see dignitaries coming from around the world to visit with your leader? Can you imagine the entire city sharing a sense of pride because your leader is so sought after by international leaders, yet he serves the best interests of your community? This was the reality in Jerusalem for a season during Solomon's reign.

My description of that model city shows you but a small part of the life its people enjoyed. That does not mean it was perfect or without its problems. Even a transformed culture does not force people to do the right things. It just makes right things easily accessible for those who have the heart to pursue them. Culture gives opportunity. It does not take away the free will of the individual. That would be a violation of God's design.

Having said that, Jerusalem was quite possibly the most transformed city in all of history, and Israel the most trans-formed nation. But it all started in the heart of Solomon's father, David, who was trained to value the presence of God as his greatest gift. All the benefits and blessings that came to the city came from the influence of that one thing.

I know such ideals seem too good to be true in this lifetime. Yet Jerusalem stands to testify to us that this is, in fact, pos-sible for those who believe. The transformation mentioned above was accomplished under the Old Covenant, at a time when the people of God did not have access to the fullness of the Spirit living in and through them, as is available for us today. How much more possible, then, is this kind of transformation in our day! For those who think such a place sounds too much like heaven, I agree. Thus it would be the fulfillment of our assignment "on earth as it is in heaven."

God Builds the Man

God always builds the individual before the individual builds the city. In this case it took two generations to set the stage for what God intended to do. In their life and ministry, David and Solomon both illustrated different dimensions of God's intentions in unique ways. They are one of the most interesting combinations in all of history. The two could not have been more different in personality or calling, yet both illustrated aspects of the life of the believer in ways that few others can. They are the perfect complement to one another.

God appeared to Solomon in a dream. It was not a theophany—an in-the-flesh visitation of God. It was a dream, and in that dream Solomon made a decision that changed the course of his life and the life of all Israel. It fascinates me that this took place while he was sleeping. God trusted him to make this monumental decision of a lifetime while he was asleep.

It was only after Solomon awoke that he realized he had been given a God moment in the middle of the night. He wrote about this principle in the Song of Solomon 5:2, when he said, "I was asleep but my heart was awake" (NASB). The spirit man does not sleep. It is able to commune with God continuously. More importantly for this story is the fact that Solomon was so devoted to the "one thing" in his life—God's purpose for him—that he could be trusted to make this important decision while he slept. That is interesting because the Lord loves to visit us in the night. In fact, some of our most profound encounters happen while we are sleeping.

We would become proud if we had the same level of encounters while we were awake, so God visits us in the night (see Job 33:15–18). God longs to fill our lives with Himself, but He will restrain Himself if doing so would in any way add to our bent for independence or pride. He truly is the ultimate steward of His grace—which is entirely for our benefit.

Self-control

Many define self-control as the ability to say no to all the distracting options we have in life. While in some measure that is true, it is better to consider this virtue as the ability to say yes to the "one thing" so completely that we have nothing left to give to the distractions. Solomon said yes to his purpose in life so completely that his devotion to this "one thing" made all other options unattractive. This approach removes us from the idea that we always have to fight to keep our priorities straight. It is not that there is no longer a fight, but this way I am fighting for something, not against something.

Solomon was absorbed with his purpose, so much so that he carried this intense focus to bed. It was no accident that God appeared to this unsuspecting young man to offer him the choice of a lifetime . . . a choice that outshines all others.

Jesus addressed this concept when He taught that if "thine eye be single, thy whole body shall be full of light" (Matthew 6:22 KJV). That is an interesting lesson. The concept here for "single" is made up of two words. The first word is the number *one*. And the second word is *voyage*. If our heart is set on *one voyage*, our body will be full of light. In other words, giving ourselves 100 percent to one purpose or voyage in life actually releases light into every other part of our life. (Notice that this metaphor addresses our body, which may provide a key to the mysterious area called *divine health*. It would be tragic to come to the end of time and have the only generation to experience divine health be Israel, in the wilderness, not even born again. Is it available to us now? I believe it is!)

David's Success

Solomon's father, David, did not succeed very well at home. He was a great king and an amazing warrior, but he failed frequently as a dad. He struggled with confronting his sons regarding their sins, thus increasing the mistrust and confusion in his household. His family situation is one of the saddest chapters in this great man's life. This one area is a study in itself that offers the student plenty of insight into *how not to raise a family*. Once again it reminds us that great people can succeed brilliantly in some areas of life, but fail completely in the area that is the most important—the home. It is true, and also sad since such failure is so unnecessary.

There was, however, one season when David did succeed as a father. It was with his son Solomon, whom his wife Bathsheba had given him. The story of David and Bathsheba gives us a profound testimony of God's grace. He extended the kingdom of His beloved David through a wife David obtained through adultery and murder. Only God could take such sin and tragedy and turn the situation around into a life-giving picture, first for an entire nation, and then for the nations of the world. The Messiah came through this lineage.

David had a vision for his son. It was a vision born of God. This was not one of those situations where a dad tries to force his plan or destiny on his child to answer his own unfulfilled dreams. This was quite the opposite. David trained Solomon to reign because he sensed the hand of God on the child's life. He trained him with purpose and taught him early in his development about this vital area called *wisdom*, the tool that enables us to *reign in life*. Solomon spoke in Proverbs 4:3–9 (NASB) of his upbringing under David and Bathsheba:

> When I was a son to my father, tender and the only son in the sight of my mother, then he taught me and said to me, "Let your heart hold fast my words; keep my commandments and live. Acquire wisdom! Acquire understanding! Do not forget nor turn away from the words of my mouth. Do not forsake her, and she will guard you; love her, and she will watch over you. The beginning of wisdom is: Acquire wisdom; and with all your acquiring, get understanding. Prize her, and she will exalt you; she will honor you if you embrace her. She will place on your head a garland of grace; she will present you with a crown of beauty."

Solomon was trained from childhood to choose wisdom above everything else. Is it possible that he was the only one God gave this choice of a lifetime to because he was the only one we know of who was trained to make the right decision? I think it is highly possible. If that is true, then what are the parallels for us as we teach the next generation? What are we drawing into the lives of our young people through our faith-filled training? In what manner are we raising the generation to come? Our prophetic decrees over them might actually attract opportunities from God. God is the ultimate steward, opening doors where they will be walked through the most.

When my children were growing up, I put them to bed by repeating these two charges night after night: "Remember, you are part of a team that is here to change the world," and, "When you go to sleep tonight, ask God if there is anything that is impossible that He wants you to do." It was my effort to raise children who know no limits.

It really does not matter if it is our children, our grandchildren or the new believers who come into our church or youth group; we must prepare them for their divine moments that unlock their supernatural destinies. We are to steward these divine moments as priceless treasures, knowing that they are not at our disposal, nor are they directed by us in any fashion. We simply serve a Father who loves His children more than we ever could. He longs for each one to discover his or her purpose as it pertains to the impossible. It is our privilege to play a role in their preparation by training the ones under our care according to faith.

Tragically, so many kill the dreams of the young in the name of realism, thinking, *We don't want these young people destroyed through disappointment.* Perhaps it is time to prepare a generation to go places we never had the time or faith to go. Some things are just worth the risk. Maybe to dream and fail is better than not to dream at all. The pursuit of a dream forms strength in someone that cannot be built up any other way. And that strength will come into play in the next season, when that person's dream is fully realized.

Desire Born of God

One of the most priceless parts of our human life is the area called desire. It is a God-given gift that separates us from all the rest of creation. The Garden of Eden was perfect in every way, yet when God placed Adam and Eve in that garden, His first command was to *be fruitful and multiply.* The command to be fruitful was not about having children, as that was inherent in the command to multiply. To be fruitful is to be productive. The Garden was perfect, but incomplete. It was lacking Adam and Eve's mark through their own creative expression. Their fruitfulness, driven by desire, would leave a mark on this place of perfect beauty.

When we keep our desires in line with the purposes of God and direct them toward Kingdom values, anything can happen. We tap in to our purpose and ensure ourselves a profound destiny. But we must guide and direct our desires according to the value of unseen realities. This is what David did right in Solomon's life. As a worshiper first, David helped attach his son's affections to an unseen world, one that is vastly superior to this world in every possible way.

In the New Testament this invisible/visible principle is found in the Sermon on the Mount. "But seek first the kingdom of God and His righteousness, and all these things shall be added to you" (Matthew 6:33). The Kingdom is the *King's dominion*, or the realm of His *domain*. This means we are to seek first the unseen reality, and then it will affect or manifest in the visible—all these things shall be added. There is no doubt that Jesus was referring to our being rewarded in the visible by seeking first the invisible. This is profoundly true. In a very real sense, this was the choice that Solomon was to make. His cry for wisdom was not a cry for material things or natural blessings. It was the pursuit of the unseen realm, which he considered of far greater value. It was this realm that had a profound effect on everything around him that was visible. His value for the unseen influenced everything. It seems appropriate that the man raised up to make such a profound choice was in fact raised by one who valued the presence of God more than life itself—the unseen over the seen.

God rewards process. He honors those who embrace principles even to the point of personal loss, for that kind of choice is what character is built on. "For wisdom is better than rubies, and all the things one may desire cannot be compared with her" (Proverbs 8:11). The only way to know if we believe that is to make the choice for wisdom in a way that costs us.

Set Up to Succeed

David wonderfully set up his son to succeed in every possible way. Yet the bottom line is that it still came down to Solomon's decisions. God appeared to him in his sleep and offered him anything he wanted. We know that wisdom was the outcome. But that was not actually what Solomon asked for, at least not directly. Solomon's choice was this:

> Therefore give to Your servant an *understanding heart* to judge Your people, that I may discern between good and evil. For who is able to judge this great people of Yours?
>
> 1 Kings 3:9, emphasis added

Solomon requested an *understanding heart*. Certainly this was the result of David's command to the child Solomon to pursue wisdom, and in the process to get understanding. But even this, as rich as it is, contains a deeper insight. The Hebrew word used here for *understanding* is the word *shama*, which means "to hear." Solomon was not asking simply for understanding; he asked for a hearing heart! In doing that, he was asking to be a well-equipped part of God's process.

God's response to Solomon is so wonderful:

Because you have asked this thing, and have not asked long life for yourself, nor have asked riches for yourself, nor have asked the life of your enemies, but have asked for yourself understanding to discern justice, behold, I have done according to your words; see, *I have given you a wise and understanding heart*, so that there has not been anyone like you before you, nor shall any like you arise after you. And I have also given you what you have not asked: both riches and honor, so that there shall not be anyone like you among the kings all your days.

1 Kings 3:11–13, emphasis added

Let me put this in my words: Solomon asked for a hearing heart, and God said, *Okay, I'll give you wisdom*. The implication is that wisdom is not just a deposit made into somebody who now has all the answers. It implies that the ability to hear the voice of God is the key to wisdom. Wisdom, then, is a relational fruit.

If the key to wisdom is hearing God's voice, then interestingly, this puts faith on similar terms with wisdom. We know that faith comes from hearing (see Romans 10:17). It does not come from *having heard*. The very nature of faith implies a present-tense relationship with God in which we are in the process of hearing Him. It is not a relationship based solely on what God has said in the past. Wisdom takes on a similar nature in that in order for it to continue functioning, we must have an ongoing relationship with God and a desire to hear His voice in our lives. This is consistent with the rest of God's word to Solomon in this exchange: "So if you walk in My ways, to keep My statutes and My commandments, as your father David walked, then I will lengthen your days" (1 Kings 3:14). In other words, God was saying, *Keep current in our relationship and I'll make sure you do great.*

The Profound Exception

Throughout history the great reformers were always people of great principle. Living according to the values of God's Kingdom and communicating those values to the people they served were all-important to them as they fully embraced the responsibility they had been given. They were patient, willing to plod when necessary to see the long-term effects of truth on the citizens of their cities. They had confidence in the power of truth. Truth declared has power. Truth declared, backed by an example, has unlimited potential. In reality, truth is attractive. No one wants to buy a car from a dishonest salesperson. In the same way, everyone longs for honesty, and ultimately for truth. What people don't want is to be controlled by religious institutions and overpowering groups of adherents. But every heart longs for truth in some measure.

It is hard for anyone who longs to impact the course of human history to feel very qualified, especially when we are lined up against people like David, Solomon, Daniel, Joseph, Esther and other historic heroes of the faith. It is challenging to think we could have the same kind of result as when God appeared to Solomon in the night and gave him anything he could ask for. That is not the experience of the average believer. Yet while it is true that Solomon had an opportunity that no one else on record has ever had with God (he could have anything he wanted), there is a profound exception to this reality. Jesus gave this same promise to everyone who follows Him:

And *whatever you ask in My name, that I will do*, that the Father may be glorified in the Son. *If you ask anything in My name, I will do it.*

John 14:13–14, emphasis added

If you abide in Me, and My words abide in you, you will *ask what you desire, and it shall be done for you.* By this My Father is glorified, that you bear much fruit; so you will be My disciples.

John 15:7–8, emphasis added

And in that day you will ask Me nothing. Most assuredly, I say to you, *whatever you ask the Father in My name He will give you.* Until now you have asked nothing in My name. *Ask, and you will receive*, that your joy may be full.

John 16:23–24, emphasis added

As only Jesus can do, He raised the high-water mark of what is possible in one person's lifetime as seen in the Old Testament by giving every one of His disciples the chance to use his or her "one wish" for the sake of humanity. Except in our case, it is not a "one wish" opportunity. This is the ongoing covenant promise He made with those who are true followers. This is the destined lifestyle of the disciple. His design is for people to help bring about His purposes on the earth through prayer and radical obedience.

The challenge in discovering our profound opportunity to have anything we want is to use this privilege for the well-being of our communities and not for building our personal empires. It would be incorrect for me to say that our personal needs are not represented in His promise. It is just that when a person has been given access to seeing nations saved and discipled, it seems small-minded to use that tool only in hopes of getting a new car. Remember, the opportunity to transform a nation was given to the one who used his God moment for the sake of the people he served. I wonder how much more God would give us if we used our moments for the sake of our city and nation.

True Wisdom

Solomon had a wisdom that is truly unparalleled in history. But he got it from Someone. His name is Jesus. Our born-again experience gives us access to a greater wisdom than even Solomon had: "You are in Christ Jesus, who became for us wisdom from God" (1 Corinthians 1:30).

The good news is that Jesus is our wisdom. The indwelling presence of Christ gives us immediate access to unequalled wisdom. On top of that, we have the admonition to pursue earnestly spiritual gifts, and that includes wisdom. God has promised to give wisdom liberally to those who ask.

My point is that although Solomon was extremely gifted of God, we have been given access to even more. We are simply without excuse.

If we can keep these things in mind and fully yield ourselves to the purposes of God for this hour, maintaining a heart of hope and promise for the days ahead, nothing will be impossible. This is our privileged moment to be alive.

5

The Nature of the Gift

Wisdom is a subject not often discussed, inside or outside the Church. We seldom hear CEOs, government leaders, health professionals or the like expressing their need for wisdom. I have heard wisdom talked about a bit more in the Church, but even then, it is a distant, abstract concept. Yet wisdom is one of the most necessary gifts God has made available for all of us to live by. Strangely, although I think wisdom is the one thing that people desire the most, they don't seem to have a language for it. Or perhaps it is that they don't have an understanding of what they need. As we display this grace from God, we awaken the latent desires in people for this priceless commodity called wisdom.

In Solomon's day, great leaders left the places where they ruled just to sit at his feet and learn from him. It is difficult for us today to understand what it took for a ruler to leave his or her place of authority, comfort and safety to become a student in another king's realm. Only a God-given hunger for wisdom could explain such a courageous move. My conviction is that a similar hunger for wisdom exists in the heart of every person in some measure. Our job as believers is to excel as servants in realms of wisdom, that the world around us might benefit and see the kindness of the Lord drawing them to repentance and relationship with Him.

Wisdom Sees Beyond

Wisdom is prophetic in nature. It functions like this: As I look at the wall here in my living room, I see a soft paint color applied to the drywall, which is nailed to wooden studs. All I can see is the paint and the drywall. But I know the drywall is attached to something I cannot see that holds it in place. Wisdom has that kind of perception, in that it sees beyond the obvious, into the internal workings of an issue, problem or design. The nature of wisdom is perceptive, understanding structures, cause and effect, and the nature of a problem and its solutions. It is the seeing gift specifically for the mind.

When people see and understand things clearly, it positions them as powerful contributors to their environment. For this reason, the wise will rise in any environment to hold the places of greatest influence. In his wonderful Passion Translation, Brian Simmons uncovers something insightful concerning wisdom and its purpose. In the introduction to his translation of Proverbs, he writes the following:

The Hebrew word for proverb, *mashal*, has two meanings. The first meaning is obviously, "parable, byword, metaphor, a pithy saying that expresses wisdom." But the second meaning is overlooked by many. The homonym, *mashal*, can also mean, "to rule, to take dominion," or "to reign with power!"

There is a deep well of wisdom to reign in life and to succeed in our destiny found within this divinely anointed compilation of Proverbs. The wisdom that God has designed for us to receive will cause us to excel, to rise up as rulers-to-be in the earth and in the spiritual realm. The kingdom of God is brought into the earth as we implement the heavenly wisdom of Proverbs![3]

In conversation, Brian told me that he feels the purpose of wisdom and the book of Proverbs is to enable us to *reign in life*. I agree completely. This understanding has helped me bring together the many loose ends that form a beautiful tapestry called *the mind of Christ*. It has also helped me understand a more practical expression of wisdom. While I never could have understood this as the twelve-year-old who chose wisdom above everything else, I now know that this piece of the puzzle is priceless. It is the concept of *reigning in life*, and it is not only an Old Testament concept. It is also mentioned in Romans 5:17 (NASB): "Those who receive the abundance of grace and of the gift of righteousness will reign in life through the One, Jesus Christ."

Reigning in life does not mean ruling over people. It is not a *Christians become all-powerful so the rest of the world can serve us* type of concept. It is quite the opposite; we become empowered to serve others well and effectively. We reign with the heart of a servant and serve with the heart of a king, all for the benefit of the people around us. Rulers in God's Kingdom never rule for their own sake. It is always for the sake of others.

3. Brian Simmons, *The Passion Translation, Proverbs: Wisdom from Above* (Racine, Wisc.: Broadstreet Publishing Group, LLC, 2014), 6.

This wonderful interpretation of the meaning of wisdom means exactly what it says. *We are to reign in life.* It means money does not rule over me through debt or greed. I rule over my finances. It means I am not defined or controlled by the conflicts I have in life. Instead, I reign through obedience to the wisdom of God's Word, until my relationships mirror the reality of heaven—or at minimum, until I have represented the heart of God in a matter. Circumstances don't rule over me. I rule over them and use them for Kingdom advantage. Wisdom gives us the power to reign.

The Coat of Favor

One of the more unique descriptions of wisdom is found in the apostle Paul's letter to the church at Ephesus:

> To the intent that now the manifold wisdom of God might be made known by the church to the principalities and powers in the heavenly places, according to the eternal purpose which He accomplished in Christ Jesus our Lord.
>
> Ephesians 3:10–11

Manifold in this verse means "multicolored." It reminds me of Joseph's coat of many colors, which spoke of the beauty of his father's favor toward him. That is what wisdom is. It carries the beauty of its source, while displaying our Father's favor toward us. In this case, as the Church displays wisdom, the unseen spiritual realm learns of God's wisdom. They are able to see firsthand that the investment Jesus made in the salvation of humanity was a wise and fruitful decision.

But not only is the Church to display wisdom in the here and now, with the entire spirit world learning from our display, it is also part of our eternal purpose. Living in wisdom for eternity is at least part of what Paul addressed in this statement to the Ephesians.

Can you imagine the redemption of humanity from an angel's point of view? Humanity, broken and lost, damned forever, and then redeemed. Not only redeemed, but also reigning in life—reigning in such a way that redeemed people remind the angels of Jesus. Wisdom is made known by the redeemed reigning in life.

Three Manifestations of Wisdom

As I read through the book of Proverbs, I notice several themes that repeatedly surface to display the nature of wisdom. Three of them are noteworthy for our study—creativity, excellence and integrity. These three areas consistently provide a measurable context in which we are to display wisdom in the practical aspects of our community life. Let's take a closer look at all three.

Creativity

Every child is an artist, but something happens as children grow up. Art becomes defined in ways that very few people excel in. That redefinition of art confines children who grew up thinking of themselves as artistic, who were always willing to take risks to express what they were thinking or seeing. As a result, they lose their spark of creative freedom. Most of the children cannot measure up to the way their parents or the educational system has defined creativity. This is tragic because we need creativity, art and beauty in every part of our lives. While not everyone can paint or sing, all of us were designed to creatively express this aspect of God's nature in and through our lives. This is wisdom. This is the liberty that Jesus brings to a life.

In Proverbs 8, wisdom is personified. This person called "wisdom" was with God on the day of creation. Several things are noteworthy in this chapter of Proverbs: wisdom delights in people; it was present as a partner in creation; prosperity and abundance are attracted to it; and it increases the favor of God upon its possessor. While we can find many more insights just in this chapter of Proverbs, the basic thing to remember for our purposes here is that wisdom is a partner to the creative process.

Wisdom is a powerful creative force that every person alive needs. The lawyer, school teacher, doctor, housewife and pastor all need to live with the freedom their own creativity provides. It is essential that we are all authentic and real in our approach to life, obviously within the context of biblical mandates. Interestingly, the place where we have the greatest freedom to express ourselves creatively is within the confines of those biblical mandates. No one who discovers who God has made him or her to be would want to be anyone else.

I have a businessman friend, for example, who never felt as though working in the business sector was a spiritual assignment. That feeling kept him from giving his all to his assigned task. But when he realized that his significance was in who called him, not in the nature of the task, he began to give himself to his business as unto the Lord. Now his measure of prosperity is hard to fathom. And for him, everything is for Jesus—everything is Kingdom—which means everyone under his influence is better off because of the favor of God resting on this man.

I read an article recently that was written by someone who has spent her life with people who are dying. When you spend time with people who are in their final months, weeks or even days of life, they tend to open up and talk about things they have been carrying in their hearts for a long time. One thing she mentioned that stood out to me was how many people regretted that they had never really become who they were on the inside, but instead had lived their lives striving to meet the expectations of others. This is the ultimate tragedy, because the world around us longs to see the authentic us. Our liberty in Christ enables us to try to be the best not just in the world but *for* the world. Fear keeps so many people from becoming who God made them to be. It is tragic for God to make so many masterpieces, only to have them compromised through the fear of man.

Creativity is normal for any believer who is not influenced by anxiety. The purest expression of our faith often can be seen in the unique way we approach life—conscious of a perfect, loving Father, and with a heart that beats to see the impossibilities of life bow to the name of Jesus through our lips. We live as people with access to heavenly solutions for earthly problems.

We were created to create. We have been called as co-laborers in the field of life, to help define the nature of the world we want to live in. Think about how God gave Adam the assignment to name the animals. Names revealed the nature of something. *Isaac* means "laughter," for example. He was the son of promise in the most impossible of circumstances. When Adam gave the animals names, he either assigned each creature a nature represented in its name, or he discerned its nature and named it accordingly. Either way, he was a co-creator in defining the world he was to live in. The Garden of Eden was perfect, in that it was without blemish. But it was not perfect in the sense of completeness until the creative touch of humanity was expressed in it.

God has given us a great capacity for providing answers creatively. Not just solutions to the world's great problems, but answers to people's desires. Answers that take us further and deeper into the purposes of God for this planet. It is the heart of our heavenly Father to meet the cries of His people's hearts. Steve Jobs, the co-founder of Apple computers, lived with the conviction that people don't always know what they want until someone shows it to them. He dreamed and worked to create products people would want, if they only knew such things existed. Henry Ford is quoted as saying, "If I had asked people what they wanted, they would have said 'faster horses.'" As these two inventors showed, wisdom is creative. It brings solutions and creative expressions that move humanity into a deeper place of experiencing the goodness and wisdom of God.

Jesus taught that it is the Father's delight to give us the mysteries of His Kingdom. The mysteries are all those things we don't know, but have legal access to as children of God. It is time to pray for ideas and witty inventions to come that will help us serve humanity in ways that express the goodness of God. It is also time to learn to tap in to new creative expression in music, on the stage, in art, in the media and through other means of communication so that we can bring our cities an awareness of having a heavenly Father who loves us. As Christians, we must get rid of the notion that the only answer for life's troubles is for us to die and go to heaven. Don't be mistaken—heaven is real and is greater than we can possibly imagine. But the kind of attitude that says rescue from this earth is the only thing we live for is an insult to the power of the blood of Jesus and the purpose of redemption.

Creativity is not a luxury item in the Kingdom. It is essential. It is portrayed as a spiritual weapon of war in Zechariah 1:18–21 (ESV):

> And I lifted my eyes and saw, and behold, four horns! And I said to the angel who talked with me, "What are these?" And he said to me, "These are the horns that have scattered Judah, Israel, and Jerusalem." Then the Lord showed me four craftsmen. And I said, "What are these coming to do?" He said, "These are the horns that scattered Judah, so that no one raised his head. And these have come to terrify them, to cast down the horns of the nations who lifted up their horns against the land of Judah to scatter it."

The four horns are spiritual powers set on destroying the people of God. God's answer to that is really quite surprising: He sent craftsmen. These craftsmen were the artistic ones, the creative ones who helped design and define the nature of the world their city was to enjoy. Not since God had sent a choir out ahead of an army going to war had He done something so unreasonable—or so it might seem to those who don't understand real wisdom and realize that its root system is in another world.

Excellence

I greatly value excellence as an expression of wisdom. I love seeing people think for themselves and tackle what is in front of them wholeheartedly. The outcome is often arresting, in that it captures everyone's attention. In one way or another, everyone has a heart for seeing the results of excellence.

Whether the expression of this value comes from the mechanic, the doctor, the housewife or the chef, it has a place in glorifying God and testifying to the true nature of wisdom.

Some of the words used to describe this *grace gift* from God are *brilliance, greatness, merit, supremacy* and *quality*. Each of these words expresses the heart given to excellence. This grace affects our productivity, our words and our relationships; in fact, it is meant to affect every area of our lives. A person who has matured in this heavenly value of excellence cannot turn it on and off at will. It becomes part of who we are and how we think.

Living a life of excellence is my offering to God. I may not be the best in the world at something, but I can always apply my best to a task for His glory. Everything we do is to be *as unto the Lord*, and done *with all our might*. This gives us the brilliant opportunity to worship God with our work. When our labor becomes our offering, it becomes like the sacrifice offered by Elijah, upon which the fire of God fell. And because *fire always falls on sacrifice*, you can see how offering God our labors draws Him into an environment in unusually powerful ways. Work can become an offering that He inhabits.

The prophet declared, "Beat your plowshares into swords, and your pruning hooks into spears; let the weak say, 'I am a warrior'" (Joel 3:10 ESV). This provides us with a unique glimpse into how God uses our natural tools of labor and makes them eternally effective by turning them into weapons of spiritual warfare. This rather abstract concept is further unveiled in the example I gave above with the horns (false authorities) and the craftsman (artisans). The creative expression these artisans offered would have little effect on society if it were not excellent. Done with excellence, our creative expressions benefit spiritual warfare. God allows our sanctified labors to become supernaturally effective in destroying the purposes and works of the powers of darkness. Perhaps this is one of the ways the Church models wisdom in such a way that the spirit world learns of His wisdom (see Ephesians 3:10).

Work done unto the Lord is sanctified work. It is set apart for His honor and attracts His manifest presence into that environment. Work done with all our might is classified as excellent work. It then becomes an expression of His nature flowing through us.

My favorite verse on this subject is Proverbs 22:29: "Do you see a man who excels in his work? He will stand before kings; he will not stand before unknown men." This teaches us two profound lessons about life. The first lesson is that kings have both an appetite and the resources to look for excellence. It is something they place God-given value on, so it is the tool God has given us to bring influence into that environment.

The second lesson reveals that excellence is the way to promotion. Excellence is the means by which people can have influence outside their normal sphere. "Kings" in our culture are often on top of the mountains of influence in business, politics, entertainment and the other areas I mentioned earlier. These people are difficult for the average person to influence, but excellence makes it possible.

Integrity

If I have a great gift for creativity and what comes from my life is excellent, but I lack character, everything is lost. Character is the glue that holds the life of wisdom in place and makes it both attractive and effective.

I ended my section on excellence with the verse from Proverbs about how excellence can bring someone before kings. That story continues in Proverbs 23:1–3: "When you sit down to eat with a ruler, consider carefully what is before you; and put a knife to your throat if you are a man given to appetite. Do not desire his delicacies, for they are deceptive food." Notice this passage says, "When you sit down to eat with a ruler . . ." Sitting down with a ruler is the assumed position of someone whose work is excellent. Excellence not only speaks to the ruler in a commercial sense, in that he wants to buy what the person produces. It goes far beyond that. The ruler is so attracted to the trait of excellence that the worker is now found eating with the king.

This is a stunning picture, and quite rare in history. I believe Joseph's story illustrates it beautifully. He resisted the temptation to sleep with Potiphar's wife, showing his integrity, and he excelled in his gift of interpreting dreams. As a result, he was brought before Pharaoh to interpret the ruler's dream. As you can imagine, Joseph must have carried himself with unusual grace for Pharaoh to promote him from prison to a place of rule overnight. Joseph ended up the number-two man in charge over all Egypt.

Those who want to live in wisdom, however, must fully embrace the warning in this Proverbs 23 passage. If we live with a high level of excellence over our lives, it will bring us before people who are outside our circle of friends and associates. This new environment will be filled with riches, power, favor and fame at a level we have never before been exposed to. The warning is to the wise: "Put a knife to your throat if you are a man given to appetite."

In other words, it is wisdom to recognize where your weaknesses lie. If you have a bent toward constantly wanting more than you have, go into the presence of a king with self-imposed restrictions. Look with honor toward the king, without being distracted by what belongs to him.

If integrity does not impact my thoughts and ambitions when I am before a king, I will end up trading my newfound place of influence for what the king possesses. I will trade the opportunity to influence for personal gain. Only integrity can keep me in the position I have gained through excellence.

The definition of *integrity* is picturesque: "unbroken completeness, totality with nothing wanting, and moral soundness." Moral soundness is a measure of integrity. It is the definition people normally use in this subject as it pertains to wisdom. But the other two definitions shed light on what happens when integrity is lacking. If it is lacking, something so necessary is missing from a person's life that it is broken, incomplete and left wanting. Integrity is an essential virtue, and it must be measurable to be proven and followed. It can be measured in people's lives by observing their moral values, the way they handle money, their speech and their relationships with other people. Integrity makes a life complete, whole and completely stable.

Integrity gives both creativity and excellence a place. It helps define the context in which these elements thrive. Tragically, society has given us many examples of creativity and excellence without integrity. These are gaudy and brash examples of what could have been. But creativity, excellence and integrity together illustrate the heart of God well.

Wisdom Flows through Love

When I think of how we can best illustrate the heart of God to the world through wisdom, I cannot help but think of the commandment Luke 10:27 (ESV) gives us on how to love God: "You shall love the Lord your God with all your heart and with all your soul and with all your strength and with all your mind."

This commandment speaks of our ability to tap in to all we are and apply it to what matters most—loving God. Every part of our being—spirit, soul and body—is an instrument through which we learn to love God. And wisdom will flow to the world through our love for Him.

The world around us is longing to see our love for God expressed in the way we serve others through the wisdom He gives us. When our love for Him is made practical through our application of wisdom in everyday life, people will see what He is like and will get a glimpse of His world. We can bring "on earth as it is in heaven" into view in the here and now as we let God's wisdom flow to the world through our love for Him.

6

The Big Test

We experience many different kinds of tests throughout life. Some tests reveal what is in our hearts and what God will be working on in us. Some tests reveal what God has already done, oftentimes without our being aware of it. Compare it to getting a flat bicycle tire fixed. First the bike shop worker puts the inflated inner tube under water to reveal the leak. Then, after he repairs the tube, he does not put it back on the bike. He reinflates it and puts it under water again, only this time the test has a different purpose. It reveals if the patch worked.

The tests we face in life fit in these two categories—those that reveal what needs to change in us, and those that prove what God has already accomplished in us—with one exception: the tests we don't know we are in. I half jokingly tell people that if they know they are in a test, it is an easy one because it is an open book test. It is the tests you don't know you are in that are the most difficult.

In 2 Kings 13:18, the prophet Elisha told the king of Israel to strike the ground with arrows. The king took arrows and struck the ground three times. The prophet became angry and told him that if he had struck the ground five or six times, he would have annihilated the enemy. But now Israel would have only three temporary victories.

I am sure the king must have wanted to take that test over once he knew what the prophet was looking for. Let's face it—it is not hard to hit the ground with arrows, a hundred times if necessary. But the prophet was not looking for the king's ability to hit the ground. He was looking for the measure of passion the king would express for his assignment even when he was not given a reason behind it. The prophet gave the king a test without providing a detailed explanation because he knew that whatever was in the king's heart would come to the surface in this assignment. Passionless leaders cost everyone who follows them.

God Protects the World

I want every person in my city to be born again. I sincerely want each person to know the hope that Jesus brings. That is a given. Salvation is the most important miracle of all. It is also the one that is the most urgent. But the conversion of every soul in my city would not solve the problems the city is facing. We would still have conflict, divorce, challenges raising children, businesses failing and issues in our school system. If you doubt that, just look at any of the churches in our city, including the one I pastor. All these issues are in the churches, too. They exist in the churches to the degree that the Kingdom does not exist there.

I remind you, the "Kingdom" is the realm of the King's dominion. Where His dominion (lordship) is lived out, there is always the expression of His world. The reason for problems in our churches is not that we are all evil people. It is simply that we have not learned the ways of the King and His Kingdom enough for Him to influence how we think and live in every part of our lives.

If I have a problem with my car, I am going to find the best mechanic I can. My first question will not be about whether or not he is a believer. It will be about the quality of his work. If I have a medical crisis, I will do the same and find the best doctor I possibly can. It would be great to have a believer for a doctor, but I will choose excellence over good intentions any day of the week.

It probably will sound a bit disrespectful when I say I believe that in some ways, God has protected the world from the Church. Of course, this is not in the sense of keeping the wonderful message of salvation from them. We have what is needed to serve the world with the Gospel of salvation. That is obviously *the great message*, with the greatest miracle of all—salvation. Our problem is that we don't always know as much about *the rest of life* as we often think we do. We tend to think that if we could just put a believer into a political office, he or she would solve all our nation's problems. I wish that were true. But once again, look at any church to see how that way of thinking actually works for us. It doesn't. In most churches, we cannot even agree on music styles, the color of the carpets and whether or not a Sunday evening meeting is necessary.

I believe it is the Lord who protects the great corporations of the world, as well as the great political offices, from the control of the Church. The reason is that we have not grown enough in our understanding of the Kingdom for Him to trust us with such places of power and influence. Put another way, the way we run the "business" of our churches would cause most corporations to collapse. It is not that evil people are involved in church, or that what we are doing does not work. Some things will work in small church settings that will not work in the bigger picture. It is just that not everything that works for us is necessarily Kingdom.

As we give ourselves to serving our city for the sake of the city—not for the sake of our ministry, our church attendance or even the church attendance across the city—we find greater open doors of influence. Let's be honest, our communities often feel that behind our desire to see people saved, we are just another religious group driven by an agenda. They see our zeal as that of a religious group trying to take over the political system to carry out its own purposes and values. And they have reason for this train of thought. We often attempt to use the political system to bring about change.

While that may seem fine on the surface, it always backfires. We cannot use the *political spirit* in one situation and think we can be free from it in another. The political spirit uses the fear of man and manipulation to get people to support a particular way of thinking. It should be obvious that such ways of thought are contrary to the Kingdom mindset. Things don't work that way. Those operating in the political systems of the world usually think differently from our King, and His Kingdom works completely differently from them. While we may try to use our political strength to bring about important changes in our country, we cannot use the same manipulative tools as those who do not know Christ. The end does not justify the means. When we operate the same way they do, we unintentionally make alliances in the spirit realm, and that realm really does not care which side of the aisle we are on, as long as we are antagonistic and dishonoring toward someone. Jesus warned in Mark 8 of the leaven of Herod. This warning was meant to open the eyes of His disciples to the snares of creating a divided allegiance in the hearts of His people. These snares are still at work to this day.

Serving a city for the sake of the city is vital. And I can testify that anyone who chooses to live this way will be tested. The very people we have come to serve are the ones who test us the most. And again, they have reason. Our cities have lived with a fear of religious agendas for decades. They do, however, welcome authentic love shown through us as we manifest real wisdom for the sake of others.

We have found that such authentic love is welcomed everywhere we have been able to offer it in our own environment. I have learned in recent years that the more we serve our city for the sake of the city—with no agenda but love, and nothing to gain personally except knowing that we have honored the Lord in how we have chosen to live—the more the city opens up to the message we carry. It is profound, and it is easy. The more we learn about how our King's world works, the greater our influence in shaping culture in this world. As we give ourselves to serve out of true Kingdom values and lifestyles, God lifts the veil of protection He has created to protect the cities from believers who are unprepared to wield such influence.

Realms of Testing

Our cities are now filled with the greatest challenges and problems I have ever seen in my life. This is the moment for believers to shine, if we will remain servants and display the kind of wisdom we see in the life of Solomon. We are being tested in many areas, but there are three in particular that will have an effect on what God is able to entrust to us in this next season. These three main realms are *favor, authority and resources.* How we do within these areas of influence will determine our impact in the decades to come.

Favor

Both David and Solomon learned something about favor that I wish were more common knowledge. David was told that God had highly favored him because of His love for Israel. This was such an obvious blessing on this royal family that the queen of Sheba recognized the same thing about David's son Solomon, saying that God had highly favored him because of His love for Israel (see 1 Kings 10:9). This has profound implications. When God gives people favor, it is because He loves those who are under their influence. That means the favor on someone has not reached its intended target until others are blessed and benefited by that favor.

People often misuse favor for self-promotion. They use it to improve their place in life, with an occasional overflow that benefits others. There is a place for realizing personal benefit through favor, but it is neither the focus of the favor nor the reason for it. It amazes me that God would give me something as personal as favor, and that it must be given away to reach its intended purpose.

Think about the implications of the queen of Sheba's statement. God gives favor to one person, making him or her extremely powerful, all because of His love for those who are around that person. This carries an important revelation for how the Kingdom works. If favor is given to me, it must benefit the people around me in order for it to be considered *favor well stewarded*. Favor that I use for self-promotion, for building my own kingdom and ministry, will fall short because it starts and ends with me. I become the Dead Sea, where everything flows in, but nothing flows out. Conversely, as I am favored, those under my influence should be better off because I am in their lives.

So why would God give me something intended for someone else? Because I share in His nature as I give. A generous lifestyle is the way of His Kingdom. My personal *self-esteem* in the Kingdom is often defined by what I do for others for their sakes.

It can also be said that God's desire for His children is to have something of their own. For this reason Jesus taught, "And if you have not been faithful in the use of that which is another's, who will give you that which is your own?" (Luke 16:12 NASB). This is called stewardship. When we use correctly that which belongs to another, we become qualified for that which is our own. This amazes me. Even though I belong to Jesus and everything I have belongs to Him, He still wants to reward me with that which is my own. The bottom line is that good stewardship is the way to increase in the things of God.

Favor is one of those heavenly commodities that we seldom pursue, study or understand. While it can be said that God loves everyone the same, not everyone has the same measure of favor. It is the reason behind one person receiving five talents, another two and another one. Remember that a talent was a sum of money, so the story about the talents in Matthew 25:14–30 is a business illustration that gives us insight into the nature and function of the Kingdom of God. Proper use brings increase. Neglect or abuse causes deep personal loss.

Favor is such an important subject that even Jesus needed it. "And Jesus increased in wisdom and stature, and in favor with God and men" (Luke 2:52). I understand why Jesus needed favor with people, since He would be eating in their homes, speaking in their cities and making disciples of them. But why would He who lived perfectly, without sin of any kind, need to increase in favor with God? I don't have an acceptable answer, but it helps me realize that if Jesus needed more favor, so do I!

One of the wonderful parts of Solomon's story was that he started his reign using his position as king correctly. God favored him and offered him a choice of anything he wanted. Solomon used his "one wish" for the sake of the people. In his mind, the people deserved a king who could make righteous decisions by hearing God's voice, decisions that would keep the citizens safe and create an atmosphere in which they could flourish. This was obvious in his request from God. It was also measurable in the results of his kingship.

Some believers make the mistake of using their favor to accuse those for whom they should be interceding. To point to the sins of the world and announce the judgment of God upon them takes no faith at all. Sin destroys everything it touches. Doom is logical. But standing in a place of prayer to bless people who don't deserve it and who cannot possibly earn it is part of the purpose of favor.

I love showing favor to everyone, but in particular I love to show extreme favor quite randomly. Occasionally, I pick someone to whom I can show unusual favor, even though I may not know the person well or know anything about his or her life. I have noticed something profound that happens as a result. When believers extend extreme favor to someone, that person rises to his or her place in life much quicker, with much more effectiveness. The person is offered open doors that were not there before, nor does it seem that those doors ever would have come. And it does not happen because people see me favoring someone and decide to follow suit. Often-times, people who know nothing about me or the kindness I have shown a certain person will choose to honor the very one I have chosen. Favor attracts favor.

We have the privilege of showing favor to people, attract-ing situations into their lives that would not come otherwise. Favor is one of the most necessary ingredients for success in the Kingdom. Using it well is what gives us access to increase.

Look at what the apostle Paul tells us: "Let no unwhole-some word proceed from your mouth, but only such a word as is good for edification according to the need of the moment, *so that it will give grace* to those who hear" (Ephesians 4:29 NASB, emphasis added). Notice that by choosing my words carefully and seeking to serve others in a way that brings them strength, I give them *grace*. This is profound. By choosing to bring strength to others with my words, I am a dispenser of grace. Grace is *divine favor*. God allows me to be a co-laborer in showing Him whom I think He should display His favor upon. And He does it! This is a correct use of favor, using it to increase God's favor upon another person's life. Once again, favor is for the sake of others. Favor attracts favor when used that way.

Never apologize for favor in your life. Favor will attract the right people to you, and it will expose the insecurities in people who might otherwise join you. Insecurity is "wrong security exposed." It is important for folks with whom you will work and minister to adequately deal with their insecurities if they are to bring real strength to what God has called you to do.

On the other hand, if you see favor on others, guard your heart from reacting with insecurity toward them, even if they seem to be getting all the breaks. And if you find people reacting badly to the favor on you, simply live your life with favor, as a servant. That makes it difficult for people to reject you forever. "When a man's ways please the LORD, He makes even his enemies to be at peace with him" (Proverbs 16:7).

Apart from Jesus, the greatest measure of favor given to someone was on Mary, His mother. The Bible says she was *highly favored.* We can take one of the more important lessons on favor from her life: Being highly favored of God does not always translate into having great favor with people. Sometimes the favor of God on people causes others to become jealous and accusatory. Not even Joseph, Mary's husband-to-be, believed her story about God getting her pregnant. Only after an angel showed up and convinced him otherwise did he honor her for the favor God had shown her. But again, you never have to apologize for favor. Use it well, and let God convince those who need convincing.

Authority

Every person has a measure of authority and is to live under authority. The authority we display is given to us according to how we respond to those God has placed over us. Many believers boast in having "all authority," but there is little in their lives to prove it. We must learn the difference between what is in our account and what is in our possession. All things have been given to me and are in my account (see John 16:15). But I am only able to use the measure I am qualified for in my surrender to God's purposes. I am "co-missioned" to the same degree I am submitted to His primary mission.

It is similar to children whose extraordinary inheritance has been measured them in smaller portions, either as they prove themselves mature enough to use it well or as they reach a certain age. The inheritance is theirs the whole time, even though they cannot always do with it what they would like. Likewise, everything Jesus owns has been given to us, but we possess only what we have the maturity to use.

We are to use our authority to uphold or restore the standard of God in a given situation. As such, we are often called to use it on behalf of those who have no voice. The heart of God, and therefore the heart of wisdom, is intensely devoted to justice, which results when authority is used well. Solomon once again illustrates this beautifully in his one wish:

> Then God said to him: "Because you have asked this thing, and have not asked long life for yourself, nor have asked riches for yourself, nor have asked the life of your enemies, *but have asked for yourself understanding to discern justice*, behold, I have done according to your words; see, I have given you a wise and understanding heart, so that there has not been anyone like you before you, nor shall any like you arise after you."
>
> 1 Kings 3:11–12, emphasis added

Authority is equally profound when we use it to validate righteous choices and uphold justice on other people's behalf. Interestingly, the first case brought before Solomon involved two harlots. Both had newborn babies, but one baby died in the night. That mother switched her child with the other. Solomon used his wisdom to find out who the real mother of the live infant was. The bigger story is that he brought justice to someone who should not have been allowed to live. Harlots were stoned to death under the Law in Israel. Wisdom displays mercy in its justice.

All authority comes from God. For us to use authority well, it must represent God accurately. This creates a whole new set of problems because people view Him so differently. There are those who see Him as an angry tyrant, and in turn represent Him that way, justifying it "biblically" the whole time. We must have at least a basic understanding of His heart and nature if we are to fulfill our assignment to transform cities and nations. Where do we start? With Jesus Christ, who is perfect theology.

Jesus used His authority to set people free. This included people who were in a mess because of their own choices. He delivered both captives and prisoners. Captives are people who are bound because of what others have done to them. Prisoners are bound because of what they have done. Jesus sets both groups free. Liberty is the product of true authority.

Many use their authority to control or manipulate others. It was the reason God warned Israel against wanting a king like other nations—because He knew these individuals would then use their authority to abuse, control and intimidate the people for the purpose of building personal empires (see 1 Samuel 8). Tragically, this tactic is sometimes used in the Church to build a personal "legacy" in ministry.

Some church leaders use their authority to keep people from sin. (They use the same tools of control, abuse and intimidation that were used by various kings throughout history.) Because this is seen as serving a good purpose, it is valued as something positive. Yet taking away people's freedom to choose is a misuse of authority, not a proper use. It is hard to correct this misuse when some consider it a virtue. Authority is to be used to serve people, period. All the graces of the Holy Spirit bring liberty. Freedom in people under my influence is the evidence that I use authority correctly.

Authority is a gift from God. Its primary function is to ensure that people are safe from evil and destruction, and in that position of safety, to ensure that each person is given opportunities to reach his or her destiny. This is the primary role of government, whether it is in the home, church or nation.

Rule with the heart of a servant, and serve with the heart of a king. This is how Jesus used His authority. Whether it was seen in His washing the feet of the disciples or casting out demons from the tormented, He used authority for others.

When I *rule with the heart of a servant*, I understand that I hold my position for the sake of others. In that context, I am looking to find opportunities to use what I have access to in God to make other people's lives better. And whatever role I have in ruling, I rule so that others thrive. When we add the supernatural element, we realize that as kings anointed to serve, we get to bring freedom to captives, recovery of sight to the blind and so on. In other words, our authority is not limited by human limitations. This is using authority well, as patterned after Jesus, the One with all authority in heaven and in earth.

When I *serve with the heart of a king*, I live with an awareness of having unlimited resources at my disposal for the sake of those around me. When we serve with our identity intact, there is no insecurity in us to undermine the role of honoring another. As royalty in God's Kingdom, we have access to realms in God simply because we know who we are. Unlike natural kings who become self-absorbed, servant kings access the storehouse of God in wisdom, revelation and understanding, including the natural resources needed for others to excel in life.

Resources

Jesus taught about money and wealth in sobering terms. He said in Mark 10:23 that it is hard for the wealthy to enter the Kingdom of God. He also taught that the love of money is a root of evil (see 1 Timothy 6:10). Sobering indeed. Yet as Jesus expanded on His word regarding the wealthy having a hard time entering the Kingdom, He added that it was an issue of trust. So the question is, how much is too much money? Political leaders around the world are trying to set that standard for us. Yet from God's point of view, it is simple. Too much money is whatever amount replaces trust.

This is an important clarification, as wisdom attracts wealth of all kinds—money, favor, opportunities, insights, revelation, knowledge and much more than could ever be listed here. It does so by God's design. Knowing the purpose and proper use of blessing is the real test of the life of obedience. Jesus told His disciples that those who left everything behind to follow Him would obtain one hundred times as much as what they gave up—*in this life* (see Mark 10:29–30).

This is quite strange. It almost feels as though Jesus is saying, "Be careful; money will kill you. And if you leave it to follow Me, I'll return one hundred times of what will kill you back into your life."

While that might be a slight exaggeration, it is not off by much. Obedience brings increase. And maintaining a heart of surrender and obedience is what enables us to handle more without letting it destroy us. Jesus is looking for people who will "love not the world," so He can entrust the world to them. In fact, we know that Jesus disciplines us that we might become more like Him. But He disciplines us so that His blessings will not kill us.

While it is a deception to think that our spirituality is proven by the abundance of our income or possessions, it is an equal error to think that it is proven by our poverty or lack. The Church has gone through seasons in which it emphasizes one or the other extreme. Reaction to error almost always creates another error. The Church has gone through seasons in which poverty and lack have been embraced as spiritual. Then in reaction to that comes a season in which wealth has been sought as the evidence of God's favor.

Israel illustrated something profound in this regard. As the people journeyed from Egypt to the Promised Land, they spent forty years in the wilderness. While their journey was never intended to take forty years, their inability to deal with their heart issues made it impossible for God to entrust this new land to them as an inheritance. The wilderness first had to become a place of complete trust in God.

When the people left Egypt, they brought all its gold with them. That should be considered a great blessing from God. But where were they going to spend their wealth in the wilderness? They turned this great sum of gold into a golden calf. All our blessings from God have the potential either to finance our purpose in Him or to become the thing we yield to in worship.

The Israelites followed the cloud of God's presence for the full forty years, until He finally took them into their inheritance. They learned that *following* was essential; it was the key to their provision and safety. Manna appeared on the ground so they could eat. Water came out of a rock so they could drink. The cloud kept them cool in the heat of the day, and the pillar of fire kept them warm at night. As long as they followed this cloud, their clothes did not wear out and they were sustained by divine health. It is a beautiful story of learning trust. But the wilderness was not God's goal for them—trust was. Their destiny was the Promised Land, where they would inherit prosperity—cities already built, with houses, crops and fully developed lands all ready to be divided up for each tribe. God had abundance in mind for His people.

Israel went without and learned to trust, and through trust, they entered their destiny. Jesus' disciples went without and learned to trust, too. But before He left them, He instructed them to get a sword. Few things better represent how to handle possessions correctly than owning a sword one cannot use. The one time Peter tried to put a sword to good use, he misused it and Jesus rebuked him. The *one hundred times as much* was their destiny, but they were to use it for divine purpose.

We must know how to steward the resources of money and opportunity well. It is nearly impossible for us to disciple leaders in the business world without having prosperity ourselves. But our prosperity must be captured by divine purpose. This is done in the way we put the money to use. Jesus taught us key concepts about that in His parables. *Talents* and *minas* are both financial currencies He used in His parables. In Matthew 25:14–30 and Luke 19:11–27, Jesus spoke of a businessman who brought his servants together to give them an assignment. In each case, the servants were to take the businessman's money and invest it well, bringing the profits to him upon his return from a long journey. The servants who brought their master increase were praised and rewarded. The servants who protected their sums of money without investing it were condemned because they brought back what they were given without profit. While these parables are about much more than money, something has to be true first in the natural before it can be used to illustrate the spiritual. Increase is not only okay; it is expected and required.

The story of the *minas* is rich in Kingdom revelation for many reasons. Jesus told this story to His disciples as an answer to what they were thinking. They were anticipating an immediate invasion of the Kingdom of God upon the earth. They were correct in seeing Jesus as King, but they were also vying for position in this kingdom they imagined, wanting to sit at His right hand and His left. For them, it would be an earthly kingdom that ruled over the cities and nations of the world. Rome would finally be put in its place, and Israel would take her rightful place as chief among mountains. (The prophets often used the term *mountains* to describe nations.)

In response to that kind of thinking, Jesus told them a story about money. In His story, the servants invested the money. As they were successful, they became leaders over cities. This is one of the most unusual promotions in the Bible. One servant turned $1,000 into $10,000 and then became the governor over a region of ten cities. Handling resources according to Kingdom values and purposes can bring about the display of God's rule over the cities of the world. That is the outcome of stewarding resources well. It is part of the responsibility of stewardship. And while my personal bent is on giving, this story applauds investing for profit.

For simplicity's sake, when we talk about how wisdom affects our resources, let's focus on three basic subjects: *generosity, possessions* and *investments*. Take a closer look with me at these three areas.

Generosity includes tithes, offerings for the work of ministry in the local church and around the world, and our efforts to take care of the poor and contribute to other social needs. While I am extremely pleased that some of the wealthiest people in the world are leading great benevolence movements to address some of the world's biggest needs, this is an area in which the Church should be leading. Not because we need to be in charge, but because we carry a mandate from God to do these things. Our problem is not usually our willingness to give, so much as it is our inability to give in equal measure to the size of the need.

In other words, these issues can only be addressed through prosperity with a purpose. The issue of poverty cannot be fixed by throwing money at the problem. But neither can it be solved without throwing money at the problem. "Abundant food is in the fallow ground of the poor, but it is swept away by injustice" (Proverbs 13:23 NASB). Those with resources must know how to solve the issues of injustice in a way that will break the systemic poverty that has kept generations from reaching their purpose and destinies. It is also vital to restore people to a place of dignity by enabling them to become contributors to society.

Possessions involve what we have. We buy clothes, homes, cars and more. Wisdom must be evident in our purchases, too. Perhaps this would be a good place to remind ourselves of what wisdom looks like—creativity, excellence and integrity. Setting these three standards in life should help us make sure that we own things that don't own us. It is not only legal to be an owner; it is essential. In owning things well, we model how to live successfully in this world while our hearts are anchored in another reigning in life.

The absolute lordship of Jesus ensures us of having blessings with no sorrows attached (see Proverbs 10:22). Pursuing wealth is a trap that guarantees much sorrow, since increase apart from the lordship of Jesus always has a price tag. Many lose their families, the trust of their friends, their good name, their reputation and so much more. It is not worth it. At the end of the day, it is not how much we possess or how much money we have in the bank; it is our family and friends, and our satisfied heart that comes from living according to His purposes.

I meet people all the time who will not drive the car they like because of what someone else will think. What a poor way to do life, reducing it to the low expectations of others. While extravagance is not the answer, neither is the fear of man. The fear of man often masquerades as wisdom. It is not. Jesus did not own much, but He did have a seamless robe—the best of His day. This is excellence.

As believers, we are to illustrate a lifestyle of contentment and abundance. It is a strange combination perhaps, but both are richly anchored in the purposes of God for His people. Through how we handle our possessions, we will become a model for a world that cannot find peace, no matter how much they buy and no matter how much they give. We can lead the charge in both realms—owning with excellence and purpose, and giving to shape the course of world history, restoring people to an identity in Christ.

Investments involve what we do with what we have. This is where we follow the examples given to us in Jesus' parables. From the parables we just talked about, we learned that it is not only legal to have increase; it is expected. At the same time, we need to be delivered from the *lottery mentality* in the Church. Many pray and hope for abundance to come into their lives out of nowhere. As a result, people often fall for get-rich-quick schemes, thinking God will bless them because they will use the money for good purposes. This is a sure formula for disaster.

God often answers our prayers for big things in seed form. In other words, instead of giving us the oak tree we asked for, He gives us an acorn. This allows us to grow along with the seed. Proper stewardship involves a process that develops someone into a steward who is able to manage increase well. Lottery winnings seldom last beyond the initial stage of big spending. Good stewardship can enable anyone to start small and end big, giving us the oak tree we asked for.

Don't invest merely for increase. Let your values play into investments. Think long-term. In other words, don't look only for profit. Look for what you want to bless and increase. Be aware that if the person managing your investments does not hold the same values you do, he or she may take you into investments you cannot justify, such as pornography. Do some research, and set boundaries for how your money will be invested.

Finally, there is nothing like good counsel. Look to God and His Word. Scripture contains sound advice for those willing to ask and seek. Also, ask God to connect you with the right people, people who are experts in this field. Try to find those who are driven by values. And while I am deeply respected by the members of our church, I would not want anyone coming to me for counsel on investments. I may have opinions, but not expertise. My opinions in this area are worth very little. I would much rather see people connect with those who have a track record of success.

Godly counsel is priceless. One thing I have noticed through the years, though, is that sometimes believers will give ungodly counsel, whereas an unbeliever will give godly counsel. Examine the counsel you are given with God's Word.

The Beauty of Giving All

One of the most wonderful stories in the Bible is of a woman who gave the ultimate expression of worship by pouring costly perfume all over Jesus (see Luke 7:37–38). Some considered it a huge waste of resources, including one of His disciples (see Mark 14:4; John 12:4–5). *Poverty of soul* always despises radical generosity.

Jesus said this woman made such a great investment that the story of her sacrifice would be spoken of throughout eternity. She gave perfume that was worth an entire year's income, and she poured it over Jesus, wiping it with her hair (see John 12:3). Here is the important lesson she showed us about what God has given us: Although she gave her perfume entirely to Jesus as an offering, and although she kept none of it back for herself, she walked out of the house smelling the same as Jesus.

When we use the favor, authority and resources given to us for God's glory and purposes, we benefit in a deeply personal way that brings delight to the heart of the Father, who loves to see His children blessed. We start smelling like Jesus, richly blessed, having *that which is our own*. Using what we have well is the big test, and when we handle this assignment well, we are given the place of influence God has designed us for since the beginning. The Old Covenant declared that God's people were "the head and not the tail" (Deuteronomy 28:13).

Israel was unable to sustain that position for very long, since they tended to focus on the blessing over the One who gave it to them. We have the opportunity to succeed where they failed by following our Lord's example and using the favor we have for the benefit of others.

7

The Power of Beauty

Wisdom embraces beauty wholeheartedly. Wisdom testifies that beauty comes forth from God. Wisdom was with God during the days of creation. All that was made was made from the influence of wisdom, bringing forth indescribable beauty as an expression of excellence. From the subdued hues of the desert sunrise to the bold display made by high mountain peaks, forests and lakes, all speak of the beauty of God. Beauty is in a baby's smile and in the song that only birds can sing. You will find it in the unending sound of waves crashing on the shore. Beauty is everywhere we turn. It is His mark upon life itself.

I wonder how many people suffer mental breakdowns only because they have forgotten how to find beauty. I love the fact that God often hides beauty so that only those in pursuit of it can find it. That must include everything from the galaxies being discovered by the scientists of our day, all the way down to microscopic phenomena. The Master Artist left His fingerprints of beauty everywhere. Beauty speaks to those willing to take the time to look.

I love the rocks called geodes. They have a common, rather drab appearance on the outside. For this reason, I call them *revival rocks*. They are unattractive on the outside, but they contain unusual beauty once they are broken open and you can see the inside. Most every great move of God is like that. It has something offensive about it at first glance, but once you see inside the movement, you discover great beauty and wonder. So much of what God made is this way. Everything seems multidimensional. Even beauty is found *line upon line, precept upon precept* (see Isaiah 28:10–13).

Beauty is everywhere wisdom has been. It helped define the many facets of creation. Even now, after so many years of abuse by humanity, the earth and all it contains radiate a glory and beauty that point to the wonder of God. The design always reflects the nature of the designer.

Wisdom illustrates beauty in creativity, excellence and integrity. Integrity is the one area seldom thought of as pertaining to beauty. Yet Scripture declares that we are to worship the Lord *in the beauty of holiness* (see 1 Chronicles 16:29; Psalm 96:9). How wonderful that holiness, the nature of real integrity, is seen as a thing of beauty. In fact, I believe all art and all creative expressions have their roots in God's nature of holiness. That is one reason it is so tragic when a person uses his or her creative energies to promote immorality, hatred or greed. These are all violations of true creativity, which has its roots in the nature of God, who is holy. All creative expressions that do not reflect Him and His nature are distortions of authentic beauty. Holiness is beautiful.

Introducing the Fullness of the Spirit

It is so easy for believers to discount the Old Testament as a part of Scripture that is no longer needed, when in reality it is the root system for all we believe and experience today. The concepts of beauty, wisdom and the fullness of the Spirit were all illustrated there before they were ever manifest in the New Covenant. One of the more interesting passages in this regard has to do with the building of Moses' Tabernacle. Both the Tabernacle and the process of building it speak volumes about the nature of God. One of the most brilliant aspects of this story has to do with whom Moses put in charge of the building and why.

> Then the LORD spoke to Moses, saying: "See, I have called by name Bezalel the son of Uri, the son of Hur, of the tribe of Judah. And I have *filled him with the Spirit of God*, in *wisdom*, in understanding, in knowledge, and in all manner of workmanship, *to design artistic works*, to work in gold, in silver, in bronze, in cutting jewels for setting, in carving wood, and to work in all manner of workmanship."
>
> Exodus 31:1–5, emphasis added

This passage amazes me for so many reasons. It deals with all areas of wisdom—excellence, creativity and integrity. *Excellence* is seen in Bezalel's gift of workmanship. In the original language, the word *workmanship* implies skill. Bezalel was chosen because of how well he had developed the gift he had, through which he glorified God. *Creativity* is acknowledged in his ability to work with different mediums to express beauty. His ability to craft artistic works in a variety of fields made him stand out to God. He could be compared to a musician who can play any instrument he picks up. It is an unusual gift. *Integrity* is here as well; Bezalel was filled with the *Holy Spirit*. Because he was a clean vessel who would not defile what he was building, he was chosen to build the Tabernacle, where the presence of God would dwell.

Beauty Saves

In his wonderful book *Beauty Will Save the World*, author Brian Zahnd recounts an important story from Church history in his prelude. A thousand years ago, Prince Vladimir the Great was looking for a new religion that might unite his people. Although he was a heathen, he recognized that spirituality might bring his people together in a common bond. He sent delegations into the neighboring countries to examine their religions and the effect of those religions on their lives. The envoy sent to examine Christianity went to the Byzantine capital of Constantinople. Below is his response to what he found:

> Then we went to Constantinople and they led us to the place where they worship their God, and we knew not whether we were in heaven or earth, for on earth there is no such vision nor beauty, and we do not know how to describe it; we only know that God dwells among men. We cannot forget that beauty.[4]

This is a testimony to the power of beauty. The words of these delegates were in response to the Christians' worship of God, and to the aesthetic beauty of the surroundings that they created in which to honor God. This beauty won the envoy's heart. Heathens were drawn to God because this

4. Brian Zahnd, *Beauty Will Save the World: Rediscovering the Allure & Mystery of Christianity* (Lake Mary, Fla.: Charisma House, 2012), xiii.

generation was given the liberty to create beauty wherever they had influence. This gift of creative expression represents the nature of God. As such, it reveals Him and has an effect on people's awareness of His heart.

We must remember that the element of beauty is highly valued by God Himself. When He speaks of the salvation of the broken, He promises to turn *ashes into beauty* (see Isaiah 61:3). Beauty is the destiny of the redeemed in every single case. Discovering what God considers beautiful will open our eyes to His work among us in profound ways, increasing our appreciation for the grace He is pouring out over people's lives all around us. It is a great privilege to celebrate the beautification process that every believer is involved in. It is real, and it prophesies that it is God's plan to bring each person into beauty as it pertains to his or her past, present and hope-filled future.

We have often mistaken the Jesus lifestyle as one that rejects beauty. Our efforts to simplify, and in some cases become rather crass in Jesus' name, have cost us immensely. We have lowered our standard of beauty that would otherwise speak of Him visually in ways that mere words cannot.

God Is a Good Father

I have heard people say that God created Adam and Eve because He needed us. That is simply not true. The Father, Son and Holy Spirit were self-contained throughout eternity, without need. God has never had any needs, only desires and wants. He knows firsthand the power of desire. All creation came into being because of His desire. That includes us. God values and desires beauty.

Even in the Garden of Eden, a place of perfect beauty, God left room for one more creative expression. God gave the first couple the responsibility to be fruitful, multiply and subdue the earth (see Genesis 1:28). As I mentioned earlier, to be fruitful was not a command to have children. That was covered in the command to multiply. To be fruitful was a command for Adam and Eve to be productive, leaving a mark even on the Garden, completing the beauty that God was looking for. God did not need their input to make the Garden complete; He wanted their input. This is His heart, the heart of a Father who longs to see the full expression of His children upon what He has made.

"Do you see a man who excels in his work? He will stand before kings" (Proverbs 22:29). Yes, that passage speaks of our influence with earthly kings—leaders in all spheres of authority and rule. But God is the ultimate King. His title is the King of all kings. The value for excellence belonged to God before it was ever imparted to earthly kings. Beauty is one of the expressions of excellence. In other words, God places an extremely high value on beauty.

God creates out of desire, not need. Thankfully, He is more than able to address our needs. Redemption is a perfect example. We needed someone without sin to die in our place, taking on Himself our punishment for sin. This is not something we could accomplish for ourselves. Jesus became Man to qualify for such a position. He lived a life without sin and died on our behalf. The debt was paid. But it was *unto* something—for a purpose beyond our adoption into God's family. As glorious as that is, there is more. God has great desires, dreams, passions and wants. And while He can make anything He wants, His dreams are connected to things that will not come into being without our cooperation. We are co-laborers in this process. The sanctity of our surrendered will illustrates His purposes beautifully. This expression of His nature is what He wants to release into the world He made.

We were created in the image of God, and having desires is part of His nature in us. He creates, builds, restores and dreams. As a result, we were created with His ability to desire. This is a unique and priceless grace He gives those made in His likeness. We have this gift because He is a Father who fulfills desires—He is the rewarder of those who seek Him (see Hebrews 11:6).

This combination of empowered dreamers desiring to express the heart of God, and the Father who longs to fulfill their desires, creates the perfect storm. But this storm is different. It is a mighty outpouring of the knowledge of the glory of God, revealing to humanity the single greatest missing truth in the consciousness of humankind—God is a Father, and He is good.

In many ways, Solomon's life illustrates what is possible through this approach to God—a Father who in every way fulfills and completes us. Solomon succeeded by using the grace he was given for the sake of those around him:

> And it came to pass, *when Solomon had finished* building the house of the LORD and the king's house, and *all Solomon's desire which he wanted to do*, that the LORD appeared to Solomon the second time, as He had appeared to him at Gibeon.
>
> 1 Kings 9:1–2, emphasis added

It was after every cry of Solomon's heart had been fulfilled that God appeared to him again. There is nothing like a profound encounter with God to increase the burning desires of our hearts for what is right and possible in our lifetime. Here is a simple question: What would it be like to come to the end of our lives and have it said of us, *"All that came into their hearts was fulfilled"*?

I remind you, selfish gratification is the opposite of what God intends by this invitation He gives us to creatively express ourselves. If we can succeed at this God-given opportunity, we will correctly illustrate the heart of God for people in a way that is both tangible and inviting. Imagine a perfect expression of the nature of God as seen through the fulfilled desires of His people. Jesus taught about this throughout John 14–16; we co-labor with God through having our desires that express His nature and will fulfilled.

One of the great misconceptions about God is that He is committed to meeting our needs, but not our wants. That concept comes in reaction to those who have taken the wonderful Gospel and made it a self-centered lifestyle, in which we use the name of God, along with His principles, to get what we want. While that is a tragic misuse of Scripture, so is the concept that God cares only for our needs. He is not the director of an orphanage, guaranteeing us three meals a day and a cot to sleep on at night. He is a Father who delights in His children by becoming involved in their dreams. He fulfills dreams and desires out of His nature. It is who He is.

The Big Surprise

The queen of Sheba traveled an incredible distance to hear and see the wisdom of Solomon. I consider this one of the most amazing yet revealing stories in the Bible. She came hoping to be impressed and left acknowledging that the half had not been told her. She also came to the conclusion that a servant in Solomon's house is better off than a king elsewhere. That is quite a summation.

The queen brought Solomon all her hard questions. I wish there were a list of the answers he gave. If nothing else, it would reveal the kind of things that were on the minds of leaders in their day. I assume her questions had to do with creation, the purpose of life and how things ought to function in God's design. I am sure there were also questions in her heart that would never cross my mind. Yet Solomon answered each one with such ease and grace that she sat mystified. Mystified at his answers? Yes. But also stunned by the life that surrounded him.

It is interesting to see what stood out to this queen as things that revealed Solomon's great creative genius—his wisdom. It is hard to explain how deeply this part of the story moves me:

> So Solomon answered all her questions; there was nothing so difficult for the king that he could not explain it to her. And when the queen of Sheba had seen all the wisdom of Solomon, the house that he had built, the food on his table, the seating of his servants, the service of his waiters and their apparel, his cupbearers, and his entryway by which he went up to the house of the LORD, there was no more spirit in her. Then she said to the king: "It was a true report which I heard in my own land about your words and your wisdom. However I did not believe the words until I came and saw with my own eyes; and indeed the half was not told me. Your wisdom and prosperity exceed the fame of which I heard. Happy are your men and happy are these your servants, who stand continually before you and hear your wisdom! Blessed

be the LORD your God, who delighted in you, setting you on
the throne of Israel! Because the LORD has loved Israel forever,
therefore He made you king, to do justice and righteousness."

1 Kings 10:3–9

This is an important passage regarding creativity and beauty.
Notice the things it mentions that caught the queen's attention, besides Solomon's brilliant answers. She saw wisdom in
*his house, the food on his table, the seating of his servants, the
service of his waiters and their apparel, his cupbearers and
the entryway by which he went up to the house of the Lord.*

If this list were not in the Bible, I doubt many of us would
have chosen these things as elements that would speak to a
queen about the nature and beauty of God. And yet they did.
The things we might consider profound did not make the
list. Solomon's explanation of nature, the purpose of life,
the location and wonder of the planets, and how the human
body works did not make it into the list that God considered
important when He inspired the writing of Scripture. Instead,
we have a house, food, serving, clothing, a food taster and
stairs that are all used to prove the wisdom of God.

Why is this so stunning? Because these are the mundane
parts of life. If God had included on the list Solomon's profound answers to life's most challenging problems, most of
us would have disqualified ourselves from the role of transforming cities and nations because we would figure our role
in life is not big enough. Apparently, there is another way
of transformation that only wisdom can see—through the
expression of beauty in the often unexciting parts of everyday life. Sometimes it is in the *stairway*, the *clothing* and the
food that the world is looking for wisdom. This becomes
the language of wisdom that the world is able to hear and

measure. This is the big surprise—that the mundane, touched by wisdom, can become an evangelistic tool.

Imagine being a woodworker who applies yourself to a life of excellence in all you put your hands to do. Because of this your reputation increases, until one day someone who represents the king contacts you and asks you to build stairs from the king's house to the house of God. Then you find out this king has an eye for design. He shows you what he has in mind, and it is truly beautiful. You receive the invitation to build under the king's charge as a gift from God, who has honored you in the sight of royalty because of your commitment to represent Him in the quality of your work. Then imagine after the project is finished, you hear more good news: A queen from another country saw the stairs you built and became convinced of God's love for people. Who would have thought that stairs could prophesy of God's love? This is beyond amazing.

Imagine being a cupbearer to the king. You obviously take your job seriously, as the king's life is in your hands. Then imagine finding out that the queen of Sheba was convinced of Israel's God because of how you approached your job with integrity, excellence and creativity. The very fact that your work was as unto the Lord brought the presence of God into the equation in a way that touched her profoundly.

Imagine being fascinated with food from childhood. Your love for complementary flavors and artistic presentation creates a reputation throughout Jerusalem. People speak of your gift. And then imagine being so committed to excellence that the king hears of your unique skills and invites you to work in the palace. Wouldn't it be the surprise of surprises to find out that the food you prepared, combined with your creative presentation, convinced a queen of the goodness of God?

I wonder what it would be like to have the job of figuring out where and how everyone should be seated at a meal with the king. This is your assignment. Excellence in you has given you an eye for details that others miss. Because it is for the king, you put extra thought into the location of the guests, the design of the table and its place settings. How would you feel when you found out later that your choice of seating and table settings spoke to a queen about how wisdom is beautiful and is filled with an order that reveals the nature of God?

These stories, and stories like them, are repeated countless times daily in communities built on wisdom. God's design for life is wonderful, victorious and prosperous for everyone. And in His design, everyone has a place to succeed and thrive. This is the beauty of wisdom. It is felt in the heart, verified by the lives of those who *reign in life* and evident in the beauty that surrounds whatever they touch. True beauty is powerful. It helped capture the heart of a queen from the south, one untrained in the ways of God . . . until Solomon . . . until she met wisdom. This is the power of beauty.

Breathless and Speechless

Not only was the queen of Sheba stunned by what she saw; Scripture says there was no more spirit in her. That word for *spirit* is also the word for *breath*. She was left breathless. It is time for the world to become speechless again. The world has a voice where the Church is silent, or worse yet, ignorant. But real wisdom captures everyone's attention, including the naysayers. When my friend and staff member Danny Silk was pursuing his master's degree in family counseling, he had to give a speech to a room full of social workers who strongly supported abortion rights. Instead of trying to win the debate through clichés and diatribes, Danny sought to express the wisdom of God on the matter. He presented his case calmly, and with great thought. At the end of his speech, the entire room gave him a standing ovation. From a position of *reigning in life*, Danny served them well from the heart of God.

We are often our own worst enemies when it comes to presenting our values and ideals to society. Besides making the mistake of partnering with the political spirit to force our opinions on society, we tend to take what works in a sermon, within a controlled audience of supporters, and use that to convince people we are right. That approach seldom works outside our church environment. It is kind of funny that we are stunned when it does not. It speaks of how out of touch we really are with the world around us. Serving others well fixes that. My dad used to say that when you wash people's feet, you find out why they walk the way they do. Serving people puts us in touch with the "whys" of their lives.

The time has come for us to think. This is part of how we love God with our minds. We need to examine how we can communicate truth in a way that the various parts of society in need of Kingdom influence will understand. I personally don't think there are many problems in our various cultures that people with true wisdom could not solve—if any. And I don't just mean the wisdom to fix problems. I mean the wisdom to present the case for truth in such a way that opponents respond with applause because they have heard more than religious rhetoric. Truth is truth, and it will stand the test of opposition.

Our Invitation

God once invited Job into a debate, which Job wisely declined. God is quite confident in His ability to convince people of truth. Together we have the mind of Christ, and we have access to the very thoughts of God about a matter. His anointing for this task of expressing truth is resting upon His people. People long to hear truth expressed with wisdom, especially when it is delivered in the context of honoring others. This is a rare combination. It is a thing of social beauty.

One of the greatest ways people are convinced of truth is by the Holy Spirit. He is released when God's people say what the Father is saying. One way to express it is that when we speak wisdom, it releases the Holy Spirit's presence into the atmosphere to work in the hearts of the listeners. This is why we have a great need for the wisdom that is based on our having a *hearing ear*. It is this ability to hear from God that makes transformation take place when we declare His words.

We are to be a generation who knows our God and can display His plans and purposes in the earth through our heart to serve and bring solutions to our communities. But beyond that, we are called to step into the privilege of bringing beauty to every part of our community life. This is our invitation for now. It happened under an inferior covenant, so it must also be possible for those in whom the Spirit of the living God now dwells.

8

What Jesus Preached

I have a pastor friend who once stood before his congregation and announced, "Today you will hear the greatest
sermon you've ever heard."

I am sure there were some who thought their preacher had
a little too much confidence in his gift that morning. But he
surprised them by reading Matthew chapters 6, 7 and 8. It is
called the Sermon on the Mount. Jesus preached this message
to a large crowd who had gathered because He had healed
their sick and had ministered to them so deeply that these
people left every responsibility behind just to spend the day
on a hillside to hear this Man. His words were life, and they
had come for life.

This sermon is rich beyond words. Jesus dealt with the
Kingdom way to happiness. He showed His listeners how
to resolve conflict and how to walk in forgiveness. He gave
them the model prayer that impacts us to this day—"on

earth as it is in heaven." In the Sermon on the Mount Jesus unveiled the revelation of what is most important in life, and as a result, seeking first the Kingdom of God became a tangible reality for His listeners. This was so significant for the Israelites as a nation. They had embraced the promise of a coming Savior, a King, the Messiah, but His coming had always been seen as a future event. For hundreds of years they had been praying for this event, and they were now spending their days listening to this One who, in their minds, just might be the One of whom the prophets spoke. It is difficult to adequately express how festive this event must have been. Miracles, His presence, joy and life-giving decrees all filled their hearts as they listened to every single word from this One who spoke like no other.

Being Salty

Let's look at a small portion of this sermon. In Matthew 5:13–14 Jesus says,

> You are the salt of the earth; but if the salt loses its flavor, how shall it be seasoned? It is then good for nothing but to be thrown out and trampled underfoot by men.
> You are the light of the world. A city that is set on a hill cannot be hidden.

Jesus is prophesying to a group of people about their purpose and destiny in God. Much like when He called Peter a *rock*, although Peter's life was more like the *broken reed* his name represented, so Jesus is calling this crowd into their potential, even though they are clueless. Just being called by God into something great makes entering that greatness possible.

For decades, I have taught on the subject of the Church being salt. Salt was used to preserve meat in biblical times, so it is not hard to understand from this illustration what effect the Church ought to have on the life of a community. Through our influence, we preserve the standard of having righteous values. While I believe this is true, it is an implied truth, or what I call a secondary message. It is not the primary lesson Jesus was teaching this group of people, although it is a concept that would stand the test against the rest of the counsel of Scripture. Jesus was teaching that salt must have *flavor* to be valuable. This is such a simple part of Jesus' message, yet I had walked past it for decades. Hearing my son Eric preach on it finally helped me understand it. The Church as a people group, not an institution, is to add flavor to the life of any city.

One of the most difficult realities for us to reconcile in our minds is that sinners liked to be with Jesus, but they are not very comfortable around most of us. It certainly wasn't that He did not believe sin was a problem. He obviously did and came to deal with its power once and for all. Yet Jesus was not afraid of being contaminated by sinfulness. As He gave Himself to touch the most broken of the world, He knew that the Life within Him was greater than any sinful influence He would face.

One of the more extreme stories that illustrates this truth is found in Mark 5:1–20, where the man of the Gadarenes, the one tormented with more demons than we could probably count, ran to Jesus, fell at His feet and worshiped. Stunning! All those demons could not keep one man from worshiping Jesus. The Church, then, is without excuse. The profound lesson modeled in this story is the man ran to be with Jesus.

His sins and torments did not keep him away, but instead caused him to draw near.

Stories of this nature are frequent throughout the four gospels. The thieving tax collector climbed a tree to get closer to Jesus, and then invited Him to his house. That was a courageous invitation, bringing into his house the One who knows everything—especially when this man was known for his deception.

Jesus' life drew sinners His way. The prostitutes, the demonized, the lepers and others who had been rejected by society all found safety in His presence. And in that safety, they found freedom from the very issues that cause many believers to avoid these groups of people yet today.

It was this Jesus who said of us all that we are to add flavor to life. Salt not only adds flavor to food; it enhances and draws out the existing flavors. While it is true that too much salt can be added to a meal, it is also true that serious health issues arise for those who have no salt.

Just one example of putting this in practical terms is that the creative musical expression released by a city's musicians should be enhanced and made more original because of the influence of the people of God. We are to add flavor. We are to have both a values-based and a presence-based influence. Because of the presence of believers, businesses should have a distinct focus and approach to serving a city well. When followers of Jesus are sprinkled throughout a community's political system, politicians should be taking on a true servant's role and dispensing hope and promise so that the citizens' skills and unique gifts are enhanced.

None of the flavorful influence Jesus' lesson alludes to results because we have taken control or have dictated to others the way things should be. We fail miserably when we resort to those tools. Success comes in part because we serve. But in a very real sense, it is simply because we are there. We become who we are in the environment of others in our community, and then the influence happens.

I have discovered that when we enjoy life with the citizens of our communities and show people that we are real and practical, we have influence. We need to have more faith and confidence in the impact that the Holy Spirit's presence in us will have. He will affect our surroundings. Like leaven worked into the entire lump of dough, we are to become immersed in the affairs of our cities. It is from that position that we have our greatest influence.

For this approach to be effective, though, we have to value people before they are converted. If we don't place value on them even though they are "pre-believers," there will be no genuine honor given in our relationships. Given correctly, honor summons people to their destiny, which ultimately can only be found in Christ.

One of the greatest examples of giving honor like this happened when Israel was coming into the Promised Land. Joshua sent two spies into Jericho, and they ended up at the house of a harlot named Rahab. She hid them from the king, who came looking for them. As a result of her kindness, the two spies made an agreement with her to guarantee her safety when Israel invaded the city. Interestingly, she told them that the people of Jericho had feared Israel ever since they heard that their God had brought them through the Red Sea—and that had happened forty years earlier.

For Rahab, this act of protection was a stunning call into the family of God. She is also honored in the great Hall of Faith in Hebrews 11, with the likes of Abraham, Moses and a list of other heroes of the faith (see verse 31). Rahab obtained salvation through her faith, which was proven by her works (see James 2:25). But what really stuns me is that after she joined the Israelites, she ended up marrying Salmon, who some think was one of those two spies sent into Jericho. In doing so, she ended up being the great-great-grandmother of King David, therefore becoming part of the Messiah's lineage.

If ever there was a message of how honor given to people before their conversion would summon them to their divine destiny, it has to be in the story of Rahab. And Jesus' lineage also included Ruth the Moabite and Bathsheba, the one with whom David committed adultery. God alone can change the impact of a life of dishonor into a life that is honorable. He alone can give hope to everyone who needs it.

In keeping with this lesson, we see an interesting moment in Scripture's commentary on Solomon receiving his extraordinary gift of wisdom. When God recorded the vastness of Solomon's wealth and wisdom, He included this bit of information in 1 Kings 4:30–31 (NASB):

> Solomon's wisdom surpassed the wisdom of all the sons of the east and all the wisdom of Egypt. For he was wiser than all men, than Ethan the Ezrahite, Heman, Calcol and Darda, the sons of Mahol; and his fame was known in all the surrounding nations.

Here God declares that Solomon's wisdom surpassed that of all others, but He then mentions Ethan, Heman, Calcol and Darda. Little else is known of these men, yet God honored them all as men who were recognized for their wisdom. Just the mention of their names in God's book stands as a testament of honor for them for all eternity. God also made sure that Scripture acknowledges the wisdom that existed in Egypt and the men of the east.

We must acknowledge what God acknowledges to fully benefit from the grace He has bestowed on others. One of the more unusual examples of this occurs in Acts 12, where it talks about Herod giving a moving speech. The people's response to his words was extreme; they cried out that his voice was the voice of a god! Herod had the ability to move people with his words:

> On an appointed day Herod, having put on his royal apparel, took his seat on the rostrum and began delivering an address to them. The people kept crying out, "The voice of a god and not of a man!" And immediately an angel of the Lord struck him *because he did not give God the glory*, and he was eaten by worms and died.
>
> Verses 21–23, emphasis added

That is a sobering story, but many miss the point: Herod's ability to move people with his words was a God-given gift. He did not die because he was called a god. He died because he did not acknowledge that it was God who had given him a moment to be *glorious* before the people. He was anointed by God to accomplish something in the earth. When he took the credit for it, however, receiving the worship of people as though he were the source of the gift, he died a painful death.

That brings us to the question, do people have a place of significance before they are converted? How is it possible for an unbeliever to write a beautiful song? How can it be that a person who lives an anti-Christian lifestyle is still a tremendous athlete? What makes it possible for a politician to give a moving speech, or a businessman to build an economic empire, before ever being saved?

In my younger years, I thought it was because the devil had inspired them. But that is giving the devil credit for something he cannot do—*create*. How, then, is all this and more even possible? It is because people are made in the image of God.

It is a privilege to recognize that everyone has been made in the image of God. Everyone deserves honor because of at least two things: They have been made in God's image, and He has given them gifts (graces and abilities) so that they can contribute to society.

Those who have surrendered their lives to Christ are due another level of honor—the Holy Spirit lives in them. "He who receives a prophet in the name of a prophet shall receive a prophet's reward; and he who receives a righteous man in the name of a righteous man shall receive a righteous man's reward" (Matthew 10:41 NASB). To *receive* someone into our lives is to recognize the gift that person has and acknowledge the way the Holy Spirit works through him or her. This is, in itself, an act of honor.

The way we receive people—acknowledge who they are and the gifts they have—also determines the deposit they will be able to make into our lives. I wonder how many people around us, both believers and pre-believers, have something to contribute to our lives, but we miss it because we cannot see God in them. It is especially challenging for most of us when we deal with the unconverted. We tend to be unable to see beyond their unconverted state, which keeps many of us from benefiting from the grace of God on their lives.

Be Bold!

Please understand that I believe in the bold preaching of the Gospel. It will always be a highly valued approach to life and ministry. It is called *overt* ministry, and it is confrontational in nature. It is commonly seen as aggressive and is expressed in great boldness. But there is also great value in the *covert* approach, which is subtle, much like the leaven Jesus referred to when He talked about the Kingdom. Leaven is quietly worked into the dough, and then the whole lump of dough comes under its influence. "He spoke another parable to them, 'The kingdom of heaven is like leaven, which a woman took and hid in three pecks of flour until it was all leavened'" (Matthew 13:33 NASB). Sin is often likened unto leaven, but in this case leaven is the Kingdom of God, the realm of His expressed dominion.

My wife, Beni, and I lived in Weaverville, California, for seventeen years, where we pastored a wonderful church called Mountain Chapel. Our only source of heat for all those years was our woodstove. I love homemade bread, and I remember so many times when the dough would sit in the pan but not rise the way it was supposed to because it was much too cold in our kitchen. Beni would take the bread and put it in front of the woodstove, and we could then watch as the change in environment activated the leaven and caused the bread dough to rise. Heat activates leaven.

It is the same in our communities. Whatever leaven has been planted—whether it is the lives of the righteous (the Kingdom), or the leaven of humanism (Herod), or the leaven of religion (the Pharisees)—it all becomes evident in the heat of difficulty or opportunity. People will choose the Kingdom over and over again when it is presented in the context of true wisdom, for wisdom brings the kind of lasting transformational fruit that everyone longs for. Thus, the goal is for the people of God to be spread throughout the systems of this world, which allows God to bring about His intended influence.

Tasteless

Jesus also spoke of salt that had no flavor. That kind of salt has completely lost its purpose and has become worthless. He went on to say that it is good for nothing and is trampled on by men. Salt without flavor has no value. In the Matthew 5:13 passage, the Greek word used for *tasteless* actually means "to make foolish." If salt without flavor is foolish, what is salt with flavor? The implied truth here is that the flavor of salt is wisdom. We add flavor to the world around us to the degree that we live in God's wisdom. In the measure we learn to reign in life and give ourselves to the pleasure and benefit of our cities, we add flavor to all we touch.

Is it possible that the picture of salt without flavor getting trampled on by men is also a picture of the Church when we live without wisdom? It would explain why in different seasons of church life believers get trampled on—because in our flavorless state our communities don't see us as valuable.

Jesus is called *the desire of the nations* (see Haggai 2:7). Jesus is the head of the Church, and we are His Body. Would it not stand to reason that if Jesus is desired by all the nations of the world, so should His Body, the Church, also be desired? Living as He did, with the purity, power, love and hope that He brought to every situation, we become necessary, too. We become desired. My goal is not political popularity. My goal is to accurately "re-present" Jesus to the world, in His most desired and necessary state. *Desired*, in that He was the friend of sinners as they sought for chances to be with Him. *Necessary*, in the way He trained people for victory, freedom and life. That is being salty. That is wisdom—reigning in life.

Useful or Necessary?

I always loved to hear the stories my parents told about when they were growing up. I loved hearing about what their lives were like and about the unique experiences they had. Hearing their stories helped create a sense of momentum in me, while at the same time giving my siblings and me a chance to laugh at some of their funny stories. My dad was a great athlete. He was injured playing high school football and required a shot before every game to numb the pain in his ankle. I think his coach was a bit frustrated with the care necessary to keep him playing, and one day he said to my dad, "Johnson, you're useful, but not necessary!"

What is the role of the Church in our cities? Are we useful, but not necessary? Our potential is obvious to us all, but we need to acknowledge the reality that we are not always viewed as necessary. We must ask ourselves what changes we need to make in order to become necessary. Consider Isaiah 62:7 (NASB): "And give Him no rest until He establishes and makes Jerusalem a praise in the earth." What would it look like for us as the community of the redeemed to become *a praise in the earth*?

One of the great stories about this in the Bible involves the time when Joseph and his family lived in Egypt. The story illustrates how it can affect a nation when someone who is considered an outsider has such impact that the nation considers him *necessary*. This is also one of the Bible's greatest stories on forgiveness and reconciliation. Although Joseph's brothers sold him into slavery, they benefited from Joseph's gift, integrity and vision.

To make a long story short, Joseph's entire family ended up residing in Egypt, living in favored status because of Joseph. Their family was highly regarded by Pharaoh himself. This regard, of course, trickled down throughout the whole nation. It was as though this world leader took it upon himself to give honor to Joseph's family for the gift he had been to this nation.

Joseph's father, Jacob, had been renamed *Israel* by God. The time came when Israel died, and Joseph naturally wept over this huge loss. Israel had been the one person in Joseph's family who had remained supportive of him throughout his life. Scripture describes the loss:

> Then Joseph fell on his father's face, and wept over him and kissed him. Joseph commanded his servants the physicians to embalm his father. So the physicians embalmed Israel. Now forty days were required for it, for such is the period required for embalming. And the Egyptians wept for him seventy days.
>
> Genesis 50:1–3 NASB

The most remarkable part of this story for me is Pharaoh's response to Joseph's loss. Not only did Joseph and his family mourn the loss of their patriarch, but so did the entire nation of Egypt. And this they did for seventy days! How is it possible for a nation to respond so deeply to the loss of an *outsider* that they mourn for seventy days? Because Jacob, Joseph and the family had become necessary to the nation.

When the days of mourning for him were past, Joseph spoke to the household of Pharaoh, saying, "If now I have found favor in your sight, please speak to Pharaoh, saying, 'My father made me swear, saying, "Behold, I am about to die; in my grave which I dug for myself in the land of Canaan, there you shall bury me." Now therefore, please let me go up and bury my father; then I will return.'" Pharaoh said, "Go up and bury your father, as he made you swear."

So Joseph went up to bury his father, and *with him went up all the servants of Pharaoh, the elders of his household and all the elders of the land of Egypt*, and all the household of Joseph and his brothers and his father's household; they left only their little ones and their flocks and their herds in the land of Goshen.

Genesis 50:4–8 NASB, emphasis added

Joseph promised to bury his dad in his homeland, not in Egypt. Pharaoh not only honored Joseph's promise; he sent all his servants, all the elders of his house and all the elders of the land of Egypt to accompany Joseph in his mournful journey. Pharaoh did not want him to be alone. How astonishing to see a world leader send his entire staff and leadership team to accompany Joseph as he kept his promise to his dad. This is a beautiful story of the impact of Joseph's wisdom upon a heathen leader and his entire nation.

The value Pharaoh placed on Jacob is legendary, and is extremely unusual throughout history. It is time to see it again, and I believe it is possible to see it in our lifetime. This should be the type of sentiment shared by those in the world when someone who has had significant impact on their lives goes home to be with the Lord. When we become those who serve well and who demonstrate the wisdom of God, we help create an appetite for God Himself.

Being Light

Besides our impact on society as salt, adding flavor to life, we are also called *light*. It would be incorrect to conclude that the light is in and of ourselves. This is one of the fascinating aspects of the significance of our conversion, because we know that Jesus is the Light that enlightens everyone who comes into the world (see John 1:9). Yet He calls all His followers *light*. We don't just reflect who He is; we radiate the nature and presence of God into the earth. We are light. Jesus spoke of this in the Matthew 5 passage we looked at earlier: "You are the light of the world. A city that is set on a hill cannot be hidden" (verse 14).

I have taught on this passage for decades, and whenever I preach on it, I emphasize the fact that light exposes things in the darkness. Once again, I see now that this is an implied truth, secondary in value. What Jesus said about us being light is much more important than what we can interpret. To illustrate the value of this light, He said, "A city that is set on a hill cannot be hidden."

One of the more forgotten truths in my circles has been that the believer living a Kingdom lifestyle is something people will come to. The background I come from has always placed heavy emphasis on the "go" of the Gospel. As a result, we are involved in sending and supporting missionaries around the world, which is one of the greatest joys of my life. Sometimes the most important gift we can give is one that cannot be measured in its eternal impact until we are actually in heaven. Missions giving is that way. In heaven, we will be able to trace the effect of every dollar given. "Going into all the world" is therefore of extreme importance to me.

But there is more. In the same way that we go to a spring to drink water . . . in the same way that we go to a tree to pick fruit . . . in the same way that we go to a building to take refuge, so we must become something that people will come to. And I don't mean come to our church services, as wonderful as that may seem. What I am really addressing is that through reigning in life, we become people who provide shelter or shade for others who realize their need. Is that not what Jesus implied? He said we are a city set on a hill. We are to be a community that people would want to come to in search of shelter and connection.

Consider the description Jesus gave us as light. We are a city. Cities don't move. This does not contradict our responsibility to take the Gospel into all the world. This is just the other side of the same coin, dealing with another aspect of this Gospel working in us. Cities that are lit up brilliantly are only seen that way when it is dark outside. The implication is that people who are outside of community, outside of personal safety and shelter, can see in the distance that there is a city ahead that may be able to help them. People will journey to that city to meet their personal needs.

The Journey to Belief

One of the more stirring statements I have heard recently is that *the disciples belonged before they believed.* As we read through the gospels, we see over and over again that they really did not know who Jesus was, even though His words and deeds had a powerful impact on them.

Eventually we do hear this statement from Peter: "You are the Christ, the Son of the living God" (Matthew 16:16). You would think that among the group of guys called to fill the significant role of becoming the original twelve disciples, this would have come up sooner. I am sure most of us would have quizzed this potential group of followers more closely than Jesus did, until we knew for sure that they agreed upon this one vitally important belief—that Jesus is the eternal Son of God. Instead, Jesus accepted them and invited them to belong, and in their journey with Him, they became believers. They belonged before they believed.

I wonder what would happen in our communities if we erased the line between *us and them* and treated people with honor before their conversion? What would it look like to become a community of believers (a city on a hill) that welcomed all travelers, knowing that some would make this city their home? It makes me wonder if we might see people come to Christ as the only possible conclusion to their journey with us of learning how to reign in life. What would it be like to have that impact on them as the ones from whom they sought shelter?

The Prophet Saw This!

On a Thursday afternoon in May 1979, I was walking and praying in the back of the sanctuary at Mountain Chapel, asking God for the *more* that He had promised. My heart ached in a way that left me entirely unsatisfied by anything less than more of Him. As I often did, I was reading the Bible and praying. For whatever reason, I happened to be in Isaiah chapter 60 that day. As I read, the words of that chapter came alive. I had learned to hear the voice of God by the reading of His Word. It had become my life. It was my practice to read and pray, and often the Scripture came alive, just as it did on that Thursday afternoon. I don't remember how long I spent before Him, but I do remember how that afternoon changed the rest of my life.

God began to speak to me through this part of Isaiah in ways I had never heard before. I began to see the role of the Church at a level that was new to me. It did not take long to realize that this insight would have great impact on my life. It would not be an exaggeration to say that this particular moment in God has affected every day of my life since then. He specifically spoke to me about Isaiah 60:1–19, although here we only need to look at the first three verses:

> Arise, shine; for your light has come, and the glory of the LORD has risen upon you. For behold, darkness will cover the earth and deep darkness the peoples; but the LORD will rise upon you and His glory will appear upon you. *Nations will come to your light, and kings to the brightness* of your rising.
>
> Isaiah 60:1–3 NASB, emphasis added

We are commanded to arise and shine. The reason is that our Light has already come. Jesus is that Light, and there is no other light coming. This is a *now* kind of command. It is disastrous when the Church takes such commands, with their promises, and puts them off into a period of time for which we have no responsibility. This is our command *now*. It is important on so many levels.

If ever there was a verse that prophesied what Jesus taught about being a city on a hill, it is this one. Not only does the prophet give the command to *arise*, he describes what will happen when we do what God said. Nations will come to our light. Is this not the city set on a hill? It is consistent with the commission of Jesus when He instructed us to disciple nations. That was not a command to get a few converts from each people group. That is a given. This command is to affect and disciple the nations of the world. When did this become a possibility? When the Light came.

It is really astonishing to see what is possible because Jesus Christ, the Light, came to earth. He is the Light that enlightens. Jesus is the radiance of the Father's glory (see Hebrews 1:3). And we are the radiance of Christ. The prophet Isaiah makes the picture quite clear: What we emanate from the Light will attract the nations to the measure that Christ is seen in us. But the prophet did not stop there. He also stated that kings would come to that same light. That tells me once again that Jesus really is the desire of the nations and that when we become all He intended, we become desirable, too. We carry something that the kings of the earth and the leaders of industry, politics, technology, medicine and every other area are longing for. We carry it. It is embedded in us, and He wants it to flow out of us until it is tangible and practical.

I am not looking for us to become famous or popular. I am looking for us to have the intended impact on culture and society that God promised and made possible. I don't want to appear before Him and discover that He put within our reach the ability to see the nations brought to Him, but because of wrong thinking, we missed our day. He deserves the nations as the reward for His suffering.

It Happened Once Before

I know of one time in history when the Isaiah 60 passage was modeled for us in a way that we can follow. It was during Solomon's reign:

> Now God gave Solomon wisdom and very great discernment
> and breadth of mind, like the sand that is on the seashore. . . .
> Men came from all peoples to hear the wisdom of Solomon,
> from all the kings of the earth who had heard of his wisdom.
>
> 1 Kings 4:29, 34 NASB

That is the closest we have ever come to fulfilling this incredible promise made by Isaiah, although that word came after Solomon's example. Perhaps Solomon's breakthrough was just a foretaste of what God originally intended. Technically, the prophecy could not be fulfilled in his time because Jesus, the Light, had not come yet. But now we have no excuse. It would be tragic to come to the end of time and see that the greatest impact on society and nations came under an inferior covenant, especially since *our Light has come!*

It makes sense to me that the men of the earth would try to sit at Solomon's feet, but I am most amazed by the fact that kings also came to sit under his influence. It was said that a servant in Solomon's presence was better off than a king elsewhere, and here we see it firsthand. Kings were known for living for themselves. It was common for kings to spend their nation's wealth on their own pleasure, comfort, safety and legacies. To sit at another king's feet meant they had to humble themselves and leave all that behind for a season. This is a sacrifice difficult for most of us to comprehend. Yet it happened day after day in Solomon's life. It came down to this: The hunger of these kings for wisdom was greater than their need for honor.

This is a startling revelation of what God has put into the hearts of leaders of all kinds—the cry for wisdom. It is ingrained in the hearts of all kings, even those we know as some of the most self-centered people on the planet. Maybe they have just never been exposed to the treasure in the field that is worth more than everything else they own, know and have become (see Matthew 13:44). Maybe all they need to see is the city set on the hill: *the city whose builder and maker is God* (see Hebrews 11:10). By reigning in life, we reveal portions of that city's blueprint.

Look at the Time!

This is our finest hour. Governments are in turmoil, cities are in confusion, as though lost, and individuals are generally without hope. What better time to live in a way that brings the keys to *reigning in life* to the forefront. These keys truly help people to live in the full effect of the Gospel of the Kingdom.

"Where there is no revelation, the people cast off restraint; but happy is he who keeps the law" (Proverbs 29:18). By carrying revelation of this nature, we are restoring humanity to the original Genesis 1:28 mandate—*be fruitful* and productive with your life by the proper use of your gifts, your legacy and your discovery of who God is. *Multiply* by having children who then have children who carry the unique legacy and heritage that is in your family line. In doing these things, we will help leave an inheritance that affects spirit, soul and body, contributing to the wholeness, well-being and heritage of entire family lines. *Subdue the earth* by first living under the rule of a Father whose love is beyond measure, and by rejecting all the inferior things that don't contribute to His purposes in the earth. Our Father God is the Father everyone longs for. Illustrating and revealing Him is the great privilege of our lives.

9

Loving Babylon

Perhaps the most unusual assignment we have been given is to love Babylon. To say that we must love it sounds almost blasphemous. Babylon stands for everything that is evil in the world and antichrist in nature. The name *Babylon* is synonymous with immorality and perversion. Yet this direction to love Babylon has a biblical basis. It is just not the focus we are accustomed to hearing about.

This concept was brought to me in one of my more interesting encounters with the Lord. It was while I was reading Jeremiah 29, the birthplace of this chapter's theme, and it took place in the same season as my Isaiah 60 encounter. Jeremiah 29 is famous for verse 11, "For I know the thoughts that I think toward you, says the LORD, thoughts of peace and not of evil, to give you a future and a hope." It is hard to get tired of reading that verse, which so clearly depicts the heart of God. He really is the Father everyone wishes they could have. But the verse that challenged my thinking was verse 7, "Seek the welfare of the city where I have sent you into exile, and pray to the Lord on its behalf; for in its welfare you will have welfare" (NASB). The word *welfare* there can be translated *well-being, health, peace* or *prosperity*. The clear instruction in this command is that there is *prosperity, well-being, peace and mental and emotional health* for you, but there is a measure you cannot have unless the city around you gets it, too. You only get what they get.

That is sobering indeed. The word *seek* also has a special emphasis, as in *seeking with care*. It implies using tools to investigate and deliberately pursue something. So we are given this mandate: to intentionally pray for and pursue, using all the tools afforded us, the health and well-being of our cities. As our cities get breakthrough, we will get the breakthroughs we need to serve the nations with our God-given mandate.

We need incredible blessing and increase to fulfill the mandate God has given us. But is it possible that blessing has been withheld from us because we want it to come to us *for* our cities instead of *with* them? We must have a love for our cities that makes us ache for their blessing, knowing it is the kindness of the Lord that leads to repentance.

It is almost as though we are afraid that if people are blessed, they will not need God. This kind of thinking has to change. It reveals so little faith in the love of a perfect Father, which wins over prodigals who are in need of His acceptance and forgiveness. Romans 2:4 still rings true—it is His kindness that leads to repentance.

My value system was challenged and shaped in my early years of pastoring. And through Jeremiah 29:7, God was addressing the bent in me toward an *us and them* approach to my city. Basically, my mindset was that there were two kinds of people in the city—those who were saved and those who were not. That may be fine as a point of theology, but it can breed attitudes in us that ruin our ability to touch the city we claim to love. No one wants to be somebody else's project, targeted especially so that a person can fulfill his or her religious duties. But that is what we have often done to our cities. We have made them projects—the targets of our ministries. It is a completely different mindset when you value people, becoming the servant of all.

Learning How to Think

For me, one of the most inspirational stories in the Bible is the life of the shepherd boy turned king—David. He gives us such profound glimpses of grace throughout his life, which is even more remarkable when you consider that he lived under the old covenant of the Law. He reformed worship, bringing music into its expression, while training a generation to value God's presence above everything else. In fact, his example of worship became the model or prototype for life in the New Testament Church (see Amos 9:11; Acts 15:16–18).

David's heart after God is legendary. Even after his deep moral failure, he became a model of how to repent deeply. He certainly was not a man without flaws. But in his weakness, he put all on the line to honor God. It could be said of David that he did everything with all his might and as unto the Lord. He succeeded in life in a monumental way.

David is an interesting study. His gift mix was extremely diverse. His passion as a musician set the standard in Scripture, yet he was simultaneously regarded as a great warrior.

He was masculinity and tenderness all wrapped up in the same body—a profound combination.

The life of this great man is one of the clearest pictures of grace I can find in the Old Testament. He illustrates realities in Christ that it is hard to imagine someone could experience prior to the cross. Yet David did. As a shepherd boy, he watched over his dad's sheep. In the wilderness alone, caring for the sheep, he learned how to be brave. He killed the lion and the bear that tried to steal from the flock. His bravery was more an expression of his trust in God than it was self-confidence, and his season as a shepherd was his training ground for becoming a man of great zeal.

David's greatest discovery had nothing to do with sheep, bravery or fine-tuning his skills as a musician. His greatest discovery was about the presence of God. He loved God and sought to honor Him with every expression he could give. His big find was all about God's response to his praise. David realized that the presence of God would inhabit his praise.

Simply put, God would establish His throne upon David's praises, showing David the kind of sacrifices that really delighted Him. This would change everything. David found in the heart of God that it was never about the blood of animals; it was about the surrendered heart. This surrender of the heart would become the pattern David established for worship in the Tabernacle once he became king. All of this was New Testament, grace-oriented living, as the people were to have no access to the actual Ark or the presence before the blood of the Lamb was shed. Yet God allowed a foretaste, that there might be a prophetic glimpse of what was to come. And that foretaste was given to David alone.

Yet in spite of the way David continuously illustrated New Testament grace before its time, he was truly an Old

Testament figure in one very clear aspect: He was a man of bloodshed. Tragically, some have used David to justify wars against unbelievers as a sign of devotion to God. This is tragic because the will of God for one season is not automatically the will of God for another season. In fact, misapplied truth often bears the fruit of a lie. The reputation of the Church suffers greatly because of this error.

Time to Build

David had a dream of building a house for God. While it may seem silly to some since God does not need a building made by man to live in, David wanted to honor Him with a building. God saw David's heart and was moved, but He would not let David build this wonderful Temple. Instead, He allowed David's son Solomon to do it:

> Then King David rose to his feet and said: "Hear me, my brothers and my people. I had it in my heart to build a house of rest for the ark of the covenant of the LORD and for the footstool of our God, and I made preparations for building. But God said to me, 'You may not build a house for my name, for you are a man of war and have shed blood.'"
>
> 1 Chronicles 28:2–3 ESV

David made a sobering discovery in his quest to build a house for God: He would not be allowed to build the Temple because he was a man of war. But God did allow David to make preparations for the building by setting aside supplies so that Solomon would have a head start. David considered his extreme generosity toward this building project a privilege—an act of worship. He prayed that the standard he set in generosity would become the standard for the people forever: "O LORD God of Abraham, Isaac, and Israel, our fathers, keep this forever in the intent of the thoughts of the heart of Your people, and fix their heart toward You" (1 Chronicles 29:18). Besides all this, David provided Solomon with elaborate plans for this Temple, plans that Solomon used and treasured.

I had always thought that not allowing David to build the Temple was God's punishment on him, much like when God would not let Moses enter the land of promise. Moses struck the rock that he was supposed to speak to, not treating the moment as holy. As a result, God would not let him enter the land promised to him. But that was not the case with David, as it was God who had made him a man of war. God directed him in battle, giving him instructions on how to fight and whom to fight. David was a mighty warrior, obtaining for Israel the lands that God had promised Joshua, but that they had never been able to obtain. And then we find that David could not build the Temple because he did what God had called him to do? God obviously could not have meant this as a punishment, for He is anything but an unreasonable Father. Instead, God was revealing an important principle: He does not build on bloodshed ministries.

Many ministries fall into the category of what I would call bloodshed ministries. They focus on destroying and tearing down instead of building up and bringing hope. When the driving force is hope, however, it changes everything. That does not mean we should not remove obstacles or correct things that are out of order. It just means that building something that will last requires that we are motivated with hope so we can build on promises. Olivia Shupe, one of the women in our church, told us some time ago, "He who has the most hope will always have the most influence."

Through the years I have watched a great number of ministries live with eternal frustration because they do not seem to be able to build something. Their frustration leads them to direct harsh words at the Church, instead of reevaluating how they should be doing ministry. The reason for their frustration? Bloodshed. Their approach to a problem is harsh and hopeless. Yet God was not punishing David by keeping him from building the Temple. He was revealing the nature of the ministry He considers suitable to build on. Bloodshed ministries make unsuitable foundations.

Biblical Murder?

The disciples even had a run-in with feeling the pressure to do bloodshed ministry. James and John wanted to call down fire on the Samaritans who would not let Jesus and His team pass through their territory. Think of it—murder was in the disciples' hearts as a solution for being rejected in ministry. The translation I use most, the New King James Version, says they justified their approach by using Elijah as an example: "Lord, do You want us to command fire to come down from heaven and consume them, just as Elijah did?" (Luke 9:54).

In His response, Jesus makes an important distinction between the ministries represented by two different covenants: "But He turned and rebuked them, and said, 'You do not know what manner of spirit you are of. For the Son of Man did not come to destroy men's lives but to save them'" (verses 55–56).

In other words, Jesus was saying, "You'll have to go to a different spirit to get that anointing, because it's not what the Father is doing today."

I wish more believers would memorize Jesus' response—*the Son of Man did not come to destroy men's lives but to save them*. It would help put an end to a lot of things done in Jesus' name that He has nothing to do with.

Not counting the bloodshed approach, there are two basic approaches to life and ministry. Both of them have had their place in history, and both of them are used as models for today. One is the model someone like Elijah exemplified. He stood outside the systems of his day and declared God's prophetic word into worlds void of God, hoping they would hear and repent. The other approach is seen in someone like Joseph, who became part of the system itself, serving others to bring about change from the inside.

I want to take a closer look at these two models, but first let me say that my intention is not to shame those who think differently than I do about how we should carry out our responsibilities. While it might seem that I am making a case for one particular model here, I have very good friends on both sides of this challenge. At a minimum, I want to raise questions so that what we do, we do intentionally, with a full understanding of our options. Biblical standards exist that support both approaches—ministry from the outside of worldly institutions or ministry from the inside.

Throughout the Old Testament, the most common form of ministry that had a powerful impact was the Elijah model. It was the right approach then, for God had ordained it for that season. This model, used throughout the Old Testament, was also John the Baptist's model. It is even used by many preachers of our day. John the Baptist came "in the spirit and power of Elijah" (Luke 1:17).

And then there is the Jesus model, which some of those who minister the Gospel today also follow. Obviously, we all would choose Jesus if we are talking about whom to follow. He alone is God, and John pointed to Him as the Light. But I refer to John the Baptist and Jesus as two separate models here for the sake of examining their approach to life and ministry, which was distinctly different.

The example Jesus provided was also illustrated at different moments throughout the Old Testament. Joseph was one who modeled this approach, and in many ways he became a model of the grace life that would unfold under the New Covenant. Given the nature of this book's message, it should be obvious that I feel the Jesus model, which was also Joseph's approach, is the one that is most vital for us in fulfilling our assignment to disciple the nations.

It's not that the Elijah/John the Baptist model is incorrect. I believe it was for a different season, though, preparing the world for the moment we are in. I believe these two models were addressed in Matthew 11, where Jesus gave tremendous honor to John the Baptist:

> But to what shall I liken this generation? It is like children sitting in the marketplaces and calling to their companions, and saying: "We played the flute for you, and you did not dance; we mourned to you, and you did not lament."
>
> For John came neither eating nor drinking, and they say, "He has a demon." The Son of Man came eating and drinking, and they say, "Look, a glutton and a winebibber, a friend of tax collectors and sinners!" But wisdom is justified by her children.
>
> Matthew 11:16–19

Jesus likened John's ministry to mourning and lamentation. He likened His own to the flute that inspires the dance. He then went on to describe the different focus He and John

139

had in their associations. John was not a socializer; he did not spend time with groups of people learning to do life together. Jesus was the opposite. He ate and drank at their weddings and feasts, and He even turned water into wine to assist at one such event. He spent time in people's homes. He ate meals with them, embraced the rejected of society and even the religious elite, and forgave the unforgivable. He concluded His comparison that we just looked at with this profound statement: *But wisdom is justified by her children.*

Our call to wisdom is a call to associate with people, mingle with them and share life together. We are to forgive them and illustrate reconciliation, while maintaining righteous standards in our personal lives. All of this, which Jesus modeled, is the call to wisdom. And wisdom has kids. The *children of wisdom* are the fruit of this approach. Those whom we serve must be the ones who help bring transformation. This happens when we do not consider this generation too dirty to touch or too dirty to serve and restore. The transformed will then become the transformers.

Wisdom Is Hearing

One of the more startling discoveries I made in my study of Solomon's life and his choice for wisdom was that for his one wish, he chose *a hearing ear.* He instinctively knew that God was the real source of wisdom, and hearing His voice would be Solomon's connection to this gift he needed. This does not mean he did not have wisdom resident in him. It just means that the source of all his wisdom was God's voice.

Many discount their ability to hear God's voice, not realizing that they could not even be born again unless they could hear. Our salvation comes down to this: God called; we responded. Hearing is at the center of our conversion. I am sure we could all say we would like to hear better, but focusing on my weaknesses never leads me to greater strength. It is much better to acknowledge the grace I am living with, in honor to the Lord, so that I can be a better steward of what He has already given me—a hearing ear.

Jesus said it rather emphatically: "My sheep hear My voice" (John 10:27). It is a fact. Hearing God's voice is part of my new nature in Christ. My confidence is not in my gifts or abilities—it is in His ability to speak loudly enough to be heard. We naturally raise our voices when we speak to someone who is hard of hearing. We take it upon ourselves to be heard. Certainly we would not think any less of God, who not only is capable of being heard by anyone, but who desires to be heard.

Jesus taught that His sheep hear His voice. This becomes the most vital part of our life in Christ. There is no other way to know His will. I know that may sound extreme, and many would remind me that the Bible declares the will of God for our lives. That is true, but consider this: The Bible gives us very clear instruction on how to think and what our values should be like. Moral decisions are very clear in the Bible. There are also many other areas of instruction that are quite clear. As a result, we know what to do in those situations. But the Bible is also famous for giving directions that appear to be contradictions. For example, should the apostle Paul go into all the world to preach the Gospel, as Jesus commissioned? Or should he avoid going into Asia, even though it is included in the "all the world" command of Jesus, but go to Macedonia instead? That is what the Holy Spirit was telling Paul to do.

We know that God is not double-minded, nor is He confusing. Yet He is willing to give us instructions that require that we have an ongoing relationship with Him if we are to know what to do. If the will of God were clear enough that we could do it without having an abiding relationship with Him, I think many people would opt for that.

Here is a favorite biblical example of contradictory instructions: "Do not answer a fool according to his folly, lest you also be like him. Answer a fool according to his folly, lest he be wise in his own eyes" (Proverbs 26:4–5). What do we do? Answer the fool, or not answer the fool? Both are commanded in this passage about how to reign in life through wisdom. The point is, we only know what to do in a given situation as we learn to hear God's voice and recognize His presence in that situation.

Think about another sobering example, the time when God told Abraham to sacrifice his son Isaac. As Abraham drew the knife back to slay Isaac, God told him to stop. I am sure Isaac was glad that Abraham kept listening to God. I wonder how many "children of promise" (fulfilled dreams) we have killed needlessly because we did not keep listening to God. It is possible to miss what He is saying because of what He has already said. Maintaining a hearing heart provides us with a great measure of safety as we pursue His will. Our ongoing relationship with God is evident in our tenderness toward the Holy Spirit. It is the absolute key for living in wisdom.

For us, hearing is essential. It is the only way to know which approach we should take at the moment: the Elijah model, as John the Baptist took, or the Jesus model, also Joseph's model. Both are rooted in Scripture. While it is not about Elijah or Joseph, it is about the schools of thought they represent. I can give you Scripture to prove Elijah's type of ministry is the most essential. And I can give you Scripture that supports

Joseph's type of ministry. But more importantly, what is the Holy Spirit emphasizing in this season? This is where there is great potential for conflict between friends on both sides, simply because of the time we have invested in a particular approach that is often out of season. Change is in the air.

Three Examples to Follow

The servant-leader remains one of the most powerful influences in the world. I chuckle at some of the instruction provided about developing leadership skills. Most of the classes and books on the topic of leadership have value, but they often ignore the principles given to us by the greatest leader of all time—the King of kings. Jesus stood with a towel over His arm and modeled how someone in a leadership role can have the greatest impact on people.

We have already talked about how in the Old Testament, Joseph serving in the world system of Egypt modeled the same approach as Jesus would later take by coming among us as a Man. Both became part of the system itself, and both served others to bring change from the inside out. It goes without saying that Jesus is our first and best example, but let's take a few minutes to look at three other examples we would do well to follow. Let's look a little more closely at Joseph, and then take a look at Daniel and Esther to see what the lives of these three tell us about becoming the leaven of the Kingdom, spreading through whatever environment God puts us in.

Joseph—Serving Someone Else's Dream

Joseph was known as a dreamer, yet his dreams were unfulfilled until he offered to serve the dream of another. It was in the role of serving Pharaoh's dream that Joseph began to see the dreams he had as a young man come to fulfillment. His example reveals the power of servant-oriented ministry, especially in leadership, where we serve to make someone else successful.

As Joseph served the revelation given to Pharaoh, who was a world leader, he single-handedly preserved the nation of Egypt in a difficult time. On top of that, he helped create a place of safety and blessing in which Israel could grow and develop as a nation. To this day, Egypt holds favored status in God's eyes for the place that country gave to Joseph and his family, who were the beginning of a nation.

God placed Joseph in an evil environment when He assigned him to Egypt. God knew that what Joseph had become on the inside made him strong enough on the outside to resist becoming like the people he served. In other words, he would not be conformed to his surroundings, but would instead have great impact on the world that surrounded him. And he did.

Daniel—Living a Different Lifestyle

This prophet of the Lord had one of the more unusual assignments ever given to a prophet. He was assigned to serve a king who was so twisted in his thinking that he killed anyone who did not worship the image he created of himself. Not only was Daniel assigned to serve this king, Nebuchadnezzar; he also was numbered with the witches, warlocks and spiritualists of his day.

Nebuchadnezzar's Babylonian kingdom was synonymous with immorality, idol worship and every evil thing. But the Babylonians also placed high value on excellence and creativity, and they gave themselves to developing a superior society surrounded by intellectualism and beauty. The Hanging Gardens of Babylon were counted among the Seven Wonders of the Ancient World. This is the world into which Daniel was planted.

Daniel's first standout decision had to do with his diet. He did not want to be defiled by eating the king's food. His overseer challenged his decision but allowed Daniel and his companions to do an experiment to make sure it would not compromise their health if they ate only vegetables. God honored Daniel's devotion and enabled him to live in great health, which was a testimony to those who knew of his decision (see Daniel 1:8–16).

This represents something of great significance for those who are called to change the system from within. My biggest concern with the *invading Babylon* approach to life and ministry is the fact that usually I cannot see any difference in the lifestyles of those who say amen to this message. It was not that way with Daniel. Even though he was working within the Babylonian system, Daniel's lifestyle was different.

What Daniel did agree to may be even more astonishing. He allowed his name to be changed from Daniel to Belteshazzar, a pagan name. He also agreed to study in the Babylonian educational system, which would include the study of occult practices. He knew that his knowledge of God's Word would keep his thought life and belief system safe. He also was convinced that what people called him would have no impact on who he was. He endured these things, but drew a line in the sand regarding his personal life. I would love to see this lifestyle followed more, as God opens the doors for more and more believers to get planted deeper and deeper in the ungodly systems of the world. But there must be a difference in their personal lifestyles.

One of my favorite stories about Daniel has to do with how he served the king in difficulty. Nebuchadnezzar had a dream about God's judgment on his life. He did not understand it, so he invited Daniel to interpret it because the "Spirit of the Holy God" was in him (Daniel 4:9). Maintaining personal holiness in an unholy atmosphere is always noticed, and is usually valued . . . eventually.

Daniel did not want to give the interpretation because the dream was against his king. But Nebuchadnezzar warned him that he needed to say what he had heard. This was Daniel's response: "My lord, may the dream concern those who hate you, and its interpretation concern your enemies!" (verse 19).

This is astonishing! How many prophets or ministers of the Gospel would have said that they wished the judgment of God, aimed at this demonized egotist, were aimed at his enemies instead? Most would basically have reminded this evil ruler that he had been warned, and that judgment upon him was past due. Tragic.

This story reveals one of the rarest types of loyalty you will ever see. Daniel's devotion to this ungodly king was based on the One who had assigned him, not the purity of the one he served. God puts us in these environments to plead the case of those whose lives have invited death through sin. When we *stand in the gap* in an intercessory prophetic role, we provide an atmosphere of safety where God's dealings will not destroy people, but instead might be instrumental in leading them to repentance. It is not because they are not guilty; it is because the discipline of God is easier to endure when there are people alongside you who truly love you.

The final scene of Nebuchadnezzar's life gives us the greatest testimony of this approach's effect. This man, who was the very example of evil kingship, stands before the Almighty—Daniel's God—and gives Him all praise and honor (see Daniel 4:37). To me, this conversion is one of the two greatest conversions in the Bible—the other being the man of the Gadarenes (see Mark 5:1–15).

Esther—Using "Carnal" Kingdom Assets

I love the fact that in the book of Esther, a woman who gained her position as queen because of her beauty spared the people of God. I don't think there is any doubt that Esther's beauty was not just outward beauty. Her king had access to the most beautiful women of the land. To stand out in that crowd, Esther would have needed the priceless combination of beauty and grace. This is true beauty, inside and out.

It is kind of refreshing to see biblical heroes use what some might consider "carnal" assets for the Kingdom. The apostle Paul used his Roman citizenship to advance the Kingdom (see Acts 16:37–40; Acts 22:25–29). He was a man of unparalleled wisdom and spiritual insight, yet it was his rights as a Roman citizen that he found the most useful in several situations. Using natural tools is not unspiritual. In some ways, it illustrates spirituality the most since it marries the two realms we are given to live in—the natural and the supernatural. It is God who merges the two into a powerful tool of transformation.

Esther was called on to use the favor given to her because of her natural beauty. Through her beauty and favor, she was able to preserve the people of God from the insane intentions of the jealous leader named Haman. Her uncle, Mordecai, was just what she needed to help inspire courage in her, but also to give her counsel and wisdom to use her moment well.

Mordecai makes one of the Bible's great statements as counsel to this queen: "Yet who knows whether you have come to the kingdom for such a time as this?" (Esther 4:14).

Esther's classic response was, "If I perish, I perish!" (verse 16).

These two comments have gone down in history as profound responses to the challenge of fulfilling our purpose. We also need courage and boldness to minister inside the systems of this world, but our courage must be laced with wisdom if we are to have our full impact on the moment God has created for us.

Being Number Two

Neither Joseph nor Daniel nor Esther was in charge of a nation. Joseph had his position because he served the dream of another with great wisdom. Daniel served from his prophetic gift, enhanced by unparalleled integrity. Esther gained influence through her beauty, which was both inside and out. With the addition of her uncle's counsel, she functioned in extraordinary wisdom. She carried a grace that marked her as a woman of destiny.

The big lesson from these three lives is that we don't need to run corporations, nations, schools or other organizations to see the influence of the Kingdom in those environments. Too often, we think it is necessary to become the leader to have influence, and we make attaining a leadership position our goal.

I suggest that it has been this passion for control in us that has brought up the defenses of the present leaders of these realms. Yet these three influencers we just looked at excelled in influence because they served well and functioned in their roles as royalty with integrity.

The Kingdom of God really is like leaven. When we introduce it into an environment as believers who know how to serve well, God proves its effectiveness in bringing transformation.

10

Erasing Lines

Honor becomes flattery when we lose sight of the power of the Gospel. Yet giving honor is vital. God does it. But it is never given to make pre-believers comfortable in their sin. It is given to woo them into the fullness of their destiny, which is impossible without a true conversion experience. To serve our cities well, we need to make some adjustments that go beyond holding an evangelistic campaign. This will affect how we think, and in turn how we serve.

It starts with how we see people. In love, God called Gideon a *mighty man of valor*, even though he was hiding from the Midianites. Jesus called Peter a *rock*, even though he lived more like the meaning of his name, *broken reed*. Jesus called Saul a *chosen vessel* before Saul ever confessed Christ and truly became a willing vessel. The apostle Paul called the believers at Corinth *saints*, even though their standards were less than saintly.

The point is, God does not flatter, but He does draw us into our purposes with words of affirmation that result in building our personal faith. We cannot get to where He is taking us without these priceless commodities called faith and love.

Fruit-Bearing Ideals

In John 15:1–4, Jesus gave us the all-time clearest instruction on having a fruitful life:

> I am the true vine, and My Father is the vinedresser. Every branch in Me that does not bear fruit He takes away; and every branch that bears fruit He prunes, that it may bear more fruit. You are already clean because of the word which I have spoken to you. Abide in Me, and I in you. As the branch cannot bear fruit of itself, unless it abides in the vine, neither can you, unless you abide in Me.

God rewards all growth with pruning. Being someone who continually hears from God is essential to remaining fruitful. The implied truth is that the good parts of our lives, the parts that bear fruit for His glory, must be pruned and disciplined. Without pruning, we will naturally develop in and grow into areas that are no longer Kingdom. Using a vine branch as an illustration, Jesus provides us with a clear picture of this. It is possible to grow beyond our fruitfulness for the Kingdom. This really is an astonishing truth. If I can put it in my own words, "Without correction, and given enough time, we can take any truth and make it have the same effect as a lie."

That may sound extreme, but you get the point. Where we are going requires constant midcourse corrections. It is impossible to aim a spaceship at the moon and have it land there without midcourse corrections. The scientists in charge of the mission know that for such a journey to be successful, constant monitoring of the spaceship's progress is required. Then and only then can there be any hope of it arriving safely on the moon. And the distance we are traveling in this Kingdom journey is far greater than the distance to the moon. Corrections and adjustments in the form of pruning are absolutely necessary for us to succeed in our assignment.

The John 15 passage deals with the fruitfulness of our lives, but I believe the principles apply to our thought life as well. In other words, there are fruitful ways of thinking and unfruitful ways of thinking. And even the ones that bear fruit need adjustment and change to continually glorify God. It is so easy for us to make assumptions based on a truth we just experienced and end up completely wrong. Assumptions must never replace the voice of God.

Romans 12:2 refers to the process called the renewing of our minds. A transformed mind transforms a person. A transformed person transforms a city. What we are all looking for in this hour does not require better tools or new Christian tricks of the trade. It requires renewed minds. That is the beginning place. In view of this, we need to take another look at three ways of thinking that we sometimes use to draw lines of separation that actually hinder our impact on the world around us.

What Lines?

Lines divide. Some division can be good. For example, dividing between a cancerous growth and the rest of the human body is an example of a good line division, made possible by the skillful work of a surgeon. But some lines keep us from fulfilling our assignment well, not because they have no theological truth behind them, but because they are misapplied, separating us from our chance to succeed in our God-given call.

I am about to address three lines that we need to erase: the line between *us and them*, the line between *the natural and the supernatural*, and the line between *the secular and the sacred*. Giving attention to the lines we are drawing in these areas will help make us more effective in our call to disciple the nations.

Us and Them

One of the most unfortunate carryovers from the Old Testament is the idea of our being contaminated by sinners and their sin. The entire Old Testament intentionally focused on the severity of sin, which is a vital revelation. Is sin still severe and devastating? Of course it is. That has not changed. But what has changed is the condition of the people of God because of the Holy Spirit within us. Plus, the nature of the Holy Spirit is different from what many have thought. Yes, He is holy, but the Holy Spirit is not afraid of sin or sinners. He illustrates how the Father thinks and what He values.

For example, God is drawn to mourning, and He promises comfort to the mourners. He is drawn to weakness, and He promises to manifest His strength in the midst of our weakness. But He is also drawn to sin, in that He declares that where sin abounds, grace does much more abound. Some of the things that offend us, He is drawn to. Seeing these things through a renewed mind, with faith in God's power to bring about change, will forever transform our approach to the world system.

The two covenants, Old and New, could not be more different anywhere than in their approach to the subject of sin and sinners. If you touch something unclean in the Old Testament, you become unclean. If something unclean touches an offering you want to give God, then the offering becomes unclean. If you touch a leper, you are defiled by his leprosy and made unclean.

Jesus changed all this, not only by promising to forgive all who came to Him, but in His approach to people who had the greatest needs. Instead of Jesus becoming unclean when touching a leper, the leper became clean when Jesus touched him! This was a sign of dramatic changes coming in life and ministry. Under the Old Covenant, we were to stay away from sinners, lest we become like them. In the New Covenant, a believing spouse sanctifies his or her entire household.

This has turned the tables completely, and we now see that the power of love and righteousness is greater than the power of sin and the influence of sinners. Instead of living in fear of contamination, we become the influencers of our surroundings. This has profound effects on how we do ministry, how we approach life and how we think.

At one time, staying away from contamination was many people's main concern. Lepers walking the streets announced their presence so as to warn people that they were coming. The blind were considered cursed by God, as Deuteronomy 28:28 declares. All these maladies in life were thought to be *from* God, and who are we to think otherwise?

This mindset caused an even greater divide between people with needs and people who should have had answers for them—the religious leaders. That was one of the offenses that

Jesus brought to all the religious elite. He was a contradiction to what they thought God was like. Jesus answered people's problems, and He showed them how to reign in life and not have their environment control them. He showed people how to get free and stay free. He opened the eyes of the ones thought to be cursed by God and calmed storms thought to have been sent by God. And then He worked to raise up a generation of believers who no longer feared contamination, but rather feared limiting God (see Psalm 78:40–43).

By removing the *us and them* approach to our cities, we stop making them ministry projects. No one would choose to be another person's ministry assignment when he or she could experience real love and acceptance in its place. That is the authentic expression of the Kingdom. Learning to get rid of the contamination approach to people, while at the same time protecting our standards of righteousness in our personal lives, gives us access to see who they really are. Seeing who God has made them to be opens our eyes to their God-given call and purpose in life. We treat them as they are becoming, not just as they are.

The Natural and the Supernatural

We live in two realms—the natural and the supernatural. God only has one realm—the natural. Everything is His natural realm. As we experience a renewed mind, we learn to see through His perspective. That is what the renewed mind is. It is the mind of Christ. This transformation of our thoughts provides a supernatural view of natural things and a natural view of the supernatural realm. This combination empowers us with a practicality that is rare in these days, and it makes us fitting for many scenarios inside and outside religious settings. That is the beauty of learning to erase this line we draw between the natural and the supernatural.

My personal bent in the last twenty-plus years has been to put an emphasis on the supernatural. I found it frustrating that there has been so little of the supernatural in Christian circles. I do not say that to blame anyone else. I was unhappy with myself, with my approach to following Jesus. I was moral, lived with principle, loved worshiping Him, loved reading and studying His Word, and had great joy in bringing people to Christ. But the miracles that Jesus illustrated were not part of my life. It was wonderful to hear of them in the lives of missionaries whom we loved and respected, and also in the heroes of the faith from many years ago or in the people who could do the big meetings. But that was not my experience. Miracles did not exist around the normal people I knew.

That sent me on a journey, one too long to write about here—except to say that watching John Wimber of the Vineyard Movement in his approach to the commission to heal the sick set me free. It was simple enough for me to mimic, until finally I was seeing the fruit I had longed to see for as long as I could remember. I am thankful to John and the whole Vineyard Movement for hosting such a wonderful manifestation of Jesus. It was and is a model I can follow.

As a church, we have intentionally focused our faith and pursuits on seeing cancer and other diseases destroyed in people's bodies. Deaf ears are opened, the wheelchair-bound get up and walk, autistic children are restored, bipolar and other brain issues are healed, and much, much more. We have had thousands of people who have been touched by the power of God experience healing and miracles in Jesus' name.

I wish I could say that everyone is healed. They are not. Everyone who came to Jesus was healed, and everyone the

Father sent Jesus to was also healed. Jesus Christ is perfect theology, and as such, He provides the only example worth following. I will not lower the standard of Scripture to fit my experience. Instead, I work to raise my level of experience to the standard of Scripture. I refuse to create another standard to give any explanation for my lack.

We have also been longing to see transformation in our city. In the process, we have discovered the need for an additional tool in our tool belt, so to speak. We need to place value on the natural. As I stated earlier, changing our thinking provides a supernatural view of natural things and a natural view of the supernatural realm. In God's Kingdom they work together, each realm complementing the other.

My favorite biblical illustration of this is in the story of Israel and the Promised Land. The people did not work for bread in the wilderness. God supernaturally provided for them. He also made sure their clothes did not wear out. They were even kept in reasonable comfort since the cloud by day protected them from the heat of the wilderness and the fire by night protected them from the cold. God took care of them. The miracles they experienced in the wilderness kept them alive. The miracles they experienced in the Promised Land gave them advancement to take the land that God was giving them as an inheritance.

As wonderful as miracles are at sustaining us in our walk with God, however, this miraculous lifestyle was not one the Israelites would typically enjoy in the Promised Land. In the land He was taking them to, they would need to work the ground, plant crops and vineyards, and raise and care for animals, knowing that the blessing of God would be on their labor to make it supernaturally effective. This would give them access to a realm of blessing they had never known—one of personal esteem that would come as a result of working as unto the Lord, seeing an abundance flow that was connected to their work and their favor with God. It was God who determined to marry the natural and the supernatural into one way of living, and this became the example of the New Testament Kingdom lifestyle.

The Secular and the Sacred

One of the countless things I am indebted to my dad for is his instruction to us that *every believer is a minister* or priest. He brought this concept to us in the early 1970s. It was first given to us in connection to the privilege of worship. Previous to this time, our tradition had sung hymns that spoke about God or addressed an important spiritual truth. But singing *to* God was unheard of in our circles.

This change took us on a journey. I will never forget the insights my dad shared about the ministry we have to God and the ministry we have to people (to the Church and to pre-believers). After my dad finished one of his messages on ministry in the inner and outer courts (from Ezekiel 44), I bowed my head and said to the Lord, "You can have the rest of my life to teach me this one thing." It had that much impact on me. I knew that I had heard something that would change the rest of my life, and I needed to make a covenant with God over this truth. It really has changed everything.

Revelation from Scripture always has many layers to it, as we were soon to discover. Being a priest in worship does not mean you are not a priest when Sunday services are over. In fact, it was becoming clearer and clearer to us that the people of God were to do the work of the ministry throughout the week (see Ephesians 4:7–13). I will never forget when my dad first presented that idea. He took a lot of heat from those locked in tradition. People thought they had hired him to do the work, and it was their job to attend, tithe and cheer him on.

No truth of Scripture comes to us by itself, without causing a domino effect in other areas of our lives. As God opens up His Word to us, it always has ramifications in other areas of our life that we thought were just fine as they were. I love it so much when God enables us to see things we have never seen before. And then when we say "amen" to what God is saying, His life flows into ours in ways we never thought possible.

The truth of the idea that *everyone is a minister* had great impact on our lives in unusual ways when my dad presented it, and still today, it is responsible for some of the greatest miracles we have seen in people's lives and in our city. I suppose one of the first things I noticed when my dad taught this principle was that people's sense of importance began to increase. The significance of the believer is an essential thing to address. God wants to increase our awareness of our personal significance. When the disciples followed Jesus, they argued about who was the greatest. Notice, however, that Jesus did not correct their desire for greatness; He just redefined it by bringing a child before them.

Those who spend time with Jesus naturally start thinking of how to have an impact on the world around them. It is significance at its finest. But if we grow in understanding our significance without remaining servants, we will move into that dangerous territory called *entitlement*, where we start thinking that we are owed blessings and favor. Once again, it is vital that *we rule with the heart of a servant, and we serve with the heart of a king.*

When I was growing up, my family had friends with all different kinds of responsibilities in our community. Some were doctors, some were business people and some were school-teachers or government workers. The people we knew filled countless roles throughout our city. The beauty that began to unfold with my dad's teaching was that people started thinking God could use them wherever they were. I grew up at a time when it was typically thought that anyone who really loved God passionately should be a pastor, a missionary or an evangelist. It was not even questioned. If someone had an unusual passion for God, it was normal to send him or her to a foreign land to serve.

I am sure there were some cases where that was the right thing to do. It is the underlying concept that I have problems with. That approach means we automatically removed our most influential and passionate people from our community life. Passion breeds passion. By sending them far away, we removed the leaven of passion from our business community, from our educational system and from the rest of our culture. How tragic and completely unnecessary. But with the idea that *everyone is a minister*, God was going after our ideas about the secular and the sacred. The notion that ministry is sacred and that work outside the Church is secular would have to change. The lines we had always drawn between the two would have to be erased.

What we have come to realize is that if you are called to be a missionary in Africa, so be it. Do it, and do it well. We will honor and celebrate the call of God on your life. But if you are called to be a medical doctor in Southern California, it is no less a call than being a missionary. The significance of the call is not found in the assignment. It is in the One who called us.

I have no desire to lower the honor we give to anyone called to the foreign field. I just want to raise the honor of all who have said *yes* to the purposes of God on their lives, wherever they serve. To fully meet the call of God on our lives requires that we live by abiding faith and that we are driven by love for God and for people. Everyone who calls on the name of the Lord for salvation is to fulfill the call of God, wherever they are.

In Acts 19 we see where "extra ordinary" miracles entered church life. What a great phrase, as it assumes that there was a level of the miraculous present that had become normal. When the Holy Spirit wanted us to realize what kind of miracles these were, He mentioned that aprons and headbands were taken from the apostle Paul's body and laid on the sick or tormented, and they were healed and delivered. During Jesus' ministry, people just touched His garment and were healed. But here the believers are taking the cloth to the sick person without the man of God being present.

This is significant in many ways, but the one important here is the fact that these were articles of clothing Paul wore as a tentmaker—in his *secular* job. These were things Paul used for the sweat of his brow and the dirt of his hands. They were not pieces of cloth that were prayed over so that people would be healed. I have no problem with that being done; we have done it and have seen God honor it with miracles. But my point is that God used the clothing Paul was wearing for what many would call *secular* work. God is the only One who can make natural labor supernaturally effective.

Absolutes

There are two absolutes in the life of a believer that have influence over every other value. We find the first one in the great love chapter, 1 Corinthians 13: "And now abide faith, hope, love, these three; but the greatest of these is love" (verse 13).

Love is *the* great call of God on a believer's life. Just being a champion of love in your community will enable you to obtain a place of influence that you could never buy. Love is measured in sacrifice, yet it carries such delight and joy that it never draws attention to the price you pay to prioritize love. You will never regret setting love as a priority.

In Hebrews 11:6, we find the second absolute for the disciple: "But without faith it is impossible to please Him." These two invaluable themes are brought together in Galatians 5:6, where Paul says that faith works through love. What makes a job secular is not the nature of the job, be it missions work or selling cars. A job is secular when we do what we do in our own strength for God, and not with God. Everything, and that includes our occupation, must be done by faith. It is a bit frightening, but there are pastors and/or missionaries whose jobs have become secular, in that they no longer need faith to do what they do. Faith must take us where we could never go on our own in our places of responsibility. If that is not happening, our job has been reduced to a secular job.

Faith keeps us fresh, dependent and on the cutting edge in our assignments. Faith is also what keeps us developing so that we can express creativity and excellence in ways that have great impact on our surroundings.

Because faith works through love, we can see that this provides the one-two punch we need for making an impact on the people around us. Love is what people want and try to get, sometimes in all the wrong places and in all the wrong ways. Real love is life-changing. And we have the privilege of establishing the climate of love over our businesses, neighborhoods and households, simply by upholding the standard of biblical love that is illustrated in sacrifice. Love costs, but the returns are eternal.

In many ways these lines we draw in our minds between *us and them, the natural and the supernatural,* and *the secular and the sacred* have kept people from the Gospel. That would never be our intention, but sadly, it is often the result. That is why we have usually thought that people needed to attend a church service to receive Christ. I love it when that happens, and I hope it never stops. But erasing these lines frees us up to display the everyday Kingdom approach to life throughout a city, so that the city itself becomes a sanctuary where salvation, healing and deliverance can take place.

Life in the Kingdom really is significantly different from what the average citizen of our cities has ever seen before. Erasing these lines brings the reality of walking with Jesus into a measurable manifestation that is both convicting and welcoming. The results are stunning. Jesus really is desirable. God is the Father everyone longs for. The Kingdom really is like leaven, influencing everything it touches.

To make the necessary changes in our thinking, we have to have greater faith in what God says will work. When we erase the lines and make the changes, that will affect what our city can see and taste through our life experience.

A Good Report

One of the most rewarding reports we have received from leaders in our city is that our people not only serve with character and responsibility; they actually influence the atmosphere over entire businesses, helping bring the owners great success. Our Bethel School of Supernatural Ministry students, as well as other people in our church, do volunteer work for our city. We even hired a man whose full-time job is to act as the liaison between the church and the city, just to manage the jobs we are given and make sure we do them with excellence. He also serves to let us know that our work is what is needed and that we are being truly effective.

The city representative who has worked with our volunteer teams has raved, almost embarrassingly so, about the integrity, love and servant hearts our people express. They have done more than they are asked, and they do it with great joy, all as an expression of love. In one example, they have saved our city well over $1 million on one project in just this past year. For a city our size, that is a substantial savings.

Without changing our view of what is spiritual and what is secular, I doubt we ever could have had such an impact in serving our city well. Now we have people in all realms of society, serving with a supernatural God, doing natural labor that God blesses in a way where His nature becomes known through their work. It is an amazing privilege and honor to love our city in this way.

11

No Devil, No Problem?

Solomon wrote a letter to King Hiram asking for his help in supplying the wood, more gold and more workers to use for building the Temple. Hiram was the king of Tyre, which was the most important port city of the Mediterranean. He had long been a friend of Solomon's father, David.

This Temple was the one David could not build because he was a man of war. He set aside most of the necessary materials in advance, however, as well as developing the plans. He did this to help his son succeed at constructing the greatest building of all time. The costs were mind-boggling. Just the silver and gold would cost considerably over $200 billion at today's prices. That does not take into account all the other materials used or even begin to touch the expense of the 153,000 laborers who worked for seven years on the project. The magnitude of the cost is simply beyond our comprehension.

The letter Solomon wrote Hiram included several fascinating points, but one thought in particular is quite possibly as mind-boggling as the expense of the building:

> You know how my father David could not build a house for the name of the LORD his God because of the wars which were fought against him on every side, until the LORD put his foes under the soles of his feet.
>
> But now the LORD my God has given me rest on every side; *there is neither adversary nor evil occurrence.*
>
> And behold, I propose to build a house for the name of the LORD my God, as the LORD spoke to my father David, saying, "Your son, whom I will set on your throne in your place, he shall build the house for My name."
>
> Now therefore, command that they cut down cedars for me from Lebanon; and my servants will be with your servants, and I will pay you wages for your servants according to whatever you say. For you know there is none among us who has skill to cut timber like the Sidonians.
>
> 1 Kings 5:3–6, emphasis added

The whole nation of Israel was wealthy at this point. Scripture says, "Also the king made silver and gold as common in Jerusalem as stones" (2 Chronicles 1:15). They did not even bother to count the silver since it was "accounted as nothing in the days of Solomon" (1 Kings 10:21). That implies wealth existed in some measure for everyone. The Israelites were also known for their artistic skills and creative approach to life.

In spite of all this, God had them involve King Hiram and his people in building the Temple. That violates some of the ideals that I grew up with regarding the help and support of people outside the faith. And here, in one of most holy events in all history, such outsiders are involved in building this holy place. Perhaps this is where Jesus' statement "he who is not against us is on our side" could find another application (Luke 9:50). It is also a testimony of God's commitment to excellence. The Sidonians were known for their skills with wood.

I love the value God places on beauty and excellence and the people who commit themselves to what He values. What has really caught me off guard is that sometimes the people who have embraced God's value for these things do not yet know Him. What a privilege we have to introduce them to the One who is the fulfillment of all they have longed for.

Here in the building of the Temple, we get another glimpse of the kind of grace where what is holy is so overwhelmingly ordained by God that the unholy cannot contaminate it. These workers were masons or those who cut wood, worked with gold or helped transport materials. They became a wonderful gift to Solomon and Israel. I find it both fascinating and beautiful that something this significant was not built by God's people alone. I wonder if maybe God wanted others to experience the joy and the shift in personal identity by being involved in something so significant. It is just like Him to do that—to allow people to discover who He made them to be through the favor He gives them to serve His purposes in something so important as building the house of God.

The part of this story I find alarming is Solomon's comment, "There is neither adversary nor evil occurrence." The word for *adversary* here is *Satan*. Was Solomon embellishing? Or was he saying the devil no longer existed in Israel? Or was he saying the devil existed, but could not cause problems? Or was he saying something completely different?

I am not sure of all the ramifications, but I am confident that Solomon was illustrating something we were later to see fully manifested in Jesus. Jesus stated that the devil had nothing in Him—no connection whatsoever (see John 14:30). We know that there was no place of agreement with the devil in any part of Jesus' life. That, of course, is expected. He is the spotless Lamb of God. But is this reality possible for us? Is it possible in a city? Is it possible for wisdom, and its corresponding grace for reigning in life, to enable people to live completely free of the enemy's influence?

If so, this reveals the profound nature and impact of true wisdom on the spirit realm. I believe to live free from the enemy's influence is not only possible, but is also absolutely necessary in order for us to fulfill our assignment. Jesus set the example—first for the individual, second for the family unit, third for a church family, and fourth and finally, for a city. The devil cannot have a place in anyone who does not give him place (see Ephesians 4:27). We give him place when we come into agreement with him by having evil plans or intentions, or when we move in fear or believe his lies.

Truth is meant to find its ultimate expression in cities and nations. Jesus addressed cities often because of what is both expected and possible in community. There are so many things in God's plan that cannot be illustrated in an individual—only in a community. Solomon, in some measure, had a similar experience to Jesus' in the sense of the devil having no place, although Solomon's experience did not last, which we will see shortly. These stories are written for our encouragement and faith, however, that we might see similar things in our lifetime.

Inheritance and Momentum

In spite of his flaws, David developed a presence-based community. His way of leadership and the values he held as a man made the presence of God his *due north*. The compass of his heart measured every decision accordingly. All of this was connected to his focus on the manifestation of God's face among His people.

Glimpses of heaven are caught throughout history, and this is one realm in which David got it clearer than almost anyone else. In heaven, the presence of God Himself is the supreme value. (When the Old Testament mentions the presence of God, it is almost always talking about His face. For example, in Moses' Tabernacle, there was the bread of His presence. Literally, that is the bread of His face.) Heaven values His face above everything there is; nothing is greater than God Himself. He is heaven—so much so that there are no shadows. In other words, He is everywhere at the same time, shining. And anytime the people of God embrace that value system, we are mirroring heaven itself. It is in part a fulfillment of the prayer "on earth as it is in heaven."

The Tabernacle of David had 24-hour-a-day worship before God's face. This was something central to David's heart and eventually to Israel as a nation. Solomon inherited this value and started his reign with this value as his personal momentum. But Solomon had a problem, which became the proverbial fly in the ointment:

Meanwhile the people sacrificed at the high places, because there was no house built for the name of the LORD until those days. And Solomon loved the LORD, walking in the statutes of his father David, *except* that he sacrificed and burned incense at the high places.

1 Kings 3:2–3, emphasis added

God's view of Solomon's love was that it was whole-hearted, with one exception. I cannot imagine anything more gratifying than having God brag on you. He recognized that Solomon loved Him and walked according to His statutes. I also cannot imagine anything more disturbing than for God to add a qualification to His description of you, as He did with Solomon's devotion—*except that he sacrificed and burned incense at the high places.* That is devastating.

High places were where the idolaters of all the surrounding nations worshiped. By climbing a mountain, we work. By getting to a higher elevation, we get closer to God. Both of these ideas represent human reasoning and self-will. While Solomon sacrificed to God, he did it outside God's directive, and he did it according to human reasoning and self-will. When we do such things, we are prone to worship *worship*, instead of worshiping God. God instructed His people's worship to take place before Him—before the Ark of His presence.

The most striking part of this problem was that God was not at the high places. He was in, upon and around the Ark of the Covenant, which was back in Jerusalem. David pitched a tent there called the Tabernacle of David, where the Ark was kept. This was where true worship had been offered to God for several decades, nonstop. The one statement that exposes what Solomon already knew in his heart, having been raised in a worship culture, was that after God appeared to him in a dream, he left the high places and came before the Ark: "Then Solomon awoke; and indeed it had been a dream. And he came to Jerusalem and stood before the ark of the covenant of the LORD, offered up burnt offerings, offered peace offerings, and made a feast for all his servants" (1 Kings 3:15).

Solomon knew. He just did not live by what he knew. This was the crack in the foundation of his reign. When God spoke to him, he instinctively returned to the Ark of the Covenant, where God's presence and glory resided, and gave offerings.

I believe some of our greatest problems take place when we live by principles and not by the presence of God. Jesus ministered out of the presence continually. The dove never left His shoulder. He remained continuously aware of His Father's voice and of what the Father was doing. David was a man of the presence. It appears to me that Solomon became a man of concept and principle instead of being an affectionate lover of the Holy Spirit.

Principles are vital. They are the result of learning how God thinks and works and how His Kingdom functions. They are to shape our way of thinking, but they were never intended to replace Him. Never is our understanding of something to replace our awareness of Him or His voice. That is where we make assumptions about God's will that look good on the outside, but are devastating in the doing.

When the construction was finally finished, Solomon had a Temple. But where was God? Where was the worship? Solomon could have continued the 24/7 approach to worship and intercession that he inherited from his father, David. But he did not. That one area of neglect cost him beyond measure.

While the Bible does not mention this, I wonder if Solomon felt any pressure to give offerings to God on the high places because that is what the people were doing. King Saul was driven by a similar value at one point in his reign.

He explained his sin to Samuel by saying, "When I saw the people were scattered from me . . ." (1 Samuel 13:11). The fear of man cripples leaders. When you are presented with a challenging decision, what is your first concern? Is it what "so-and-so" will think? Solomon saw the people worshiping at the high places and perhaps wanted to have great favor with them, so he joined them.

If we don't live by the praises of men, we will not die by their criticisms. It is important to give honor and respect to all people, but my obedience belongs to God alone. Even my obedience to civil government is as unto the Lord, as it is His command for me.

Man of Peace

Solomon grew up knowing his call and purpose in life. He was groomed to reign, and his reign was defined prophetically. Unlike his father, David, who lived a life of war, Solomon would reign in peace.

> Behold, a son shall be born to you, who shall be a man of rest; and I will give him rest from all his enemies all around. His name shall be Solomon, for I will give peace and quietness to Israel in his days. He shall build a house for My name, and he shall be My son, and I will be his Father; and I will establish the throne of his kingdom over Israel forever.
>
> 1 Chronicles 22:9–10

This was the word the Lord spoke to David before Solomon was ever born. This promise no doubt shaped how Solomon was raised and what was spoken over his life while he grew up. It is important that we raise our children with a sense of destiny, but without trying to control or manipulate them into fulfilling the dreams we have for them. Theirs must be a God-given destiny. And even then, it is not subject to our interpretation. The Scripture says to raise our children *in the way they should go* (see Proverbs 22:6). That is not necessarily the same as how we think they should go. David was a man with a dream. As a result, he raised a son with a destiny. I feel sorry for children who are raised in homes without dreams.

Here is David's personal charge to his son about his need for wisdom, his assignment to build the house of the Lord and the absolute necessity of living with courage:

> Now, my son, may the LORD be with you; and may you prosper, and build the house of the LORD your God, as He has said to you. Only may the Lord give you wisdom and understanding, and give you charge concerning Israel, that you may keep the law of the LORD your God. Then you will prosper, if you take care to fulfill the statutes and judgments with which the LORD charged Moses concerning Israel. Be strong and of good courage; do not fear nor be dismayed.
>
> 1 Chronicles 22:11–13

It might seem strange to some that a man of peace should need courage, but it is true. Maintaining God's type of peace requires great courage. This may be where things began to break down for Solomon. He reduced peace to treaties, and unlawful ones at that:

> Now Solomon made a treaty with Pharaoh king of Egypt, and married Pharaoh's daughter; then he brought her to the City of David until he had finished building his own house, and the house of the LORD, and the wall all around Jerusalem.
>
> 1 Kings 3:1

Is it possible that this treaty and marriage, which God did not direct, opened the door for Israel as a nation to move into compromise in their worship? This is the event that led the people to offer sacrifices on the high places. Israelites were forbidden to marry foreign wives since such women worshiped other gods. God warned Israel that they would end up worshiping false gods as a result of such unions. Solomon apparently thought he could handle the temptation, but not even wisdom could protect him from this impending failure—especially if he was not going to use that wisdom.

It is doubtful that David ever allowed compromise in worship while he was king. There is no mention of it, as there is with Solomon. Worshiping on the high places and making treaties to keep the peace are both the efforts of man to accomplish Kingdom purposes. They don't work, at least not in a way that has eternal value and purpose.

The Lower Standard Wins

In the days of the Old Testament, it was easier to be influenced toward evil than it was to be influenced toward good, as the Holy Spirit was not yet dwelling in His people. (When the Holy Spirit dwells in people, He changes their nature. This new nature has a bent toward righteousness.) Such was the case for Solomon as he sought to build a kingdom of peace. But peace at any cost is no longer peace.

When God creates peace, it is based on the presence of a Person called the Prince of Peace. That peace also has a military effect: "And the God of peace will crush Satan under your feet" (Romans 16:20). Outside the Kingdom of God, peace is the absence of something, whereas in the Kingdom of God, it is the presence of Someone.

Solomon was building the inferior type of peace by making treaties that God did not direct and that would give place to compromise. He valued the absence of war as evidence of the success of his reign. It was a false success.

In many ways Solomon never became a man of true peace, at least not in the Kingdom sense. His peace was found in treaties and in the absence of war. But he never became a presence-oriented person, as was his father, David. David lived from the presence of God. Even in his moral failure, his cry was, "Do not take your Holy Spirit from me" (Psalm 51:11). But there is no evidence that Solomon was a worshiper of God, at least not in the same way as David was. It was not a requirement that he become a musician like his father; that is not everyone's gift. But everyone should be a worshiper.

The higher we rise in favor and authority, the more devastating the effects of our compromising decisions. So it was for Solomon. Imagine a building whose foundation is an inch lower on one side than on the other. If the building is a story or two tall, it is not much of a problem. But build a hundred-story building with that one-inch mistake in the foundation, and you have major problems. The tilt in the building will create unbearable pressure on the building materials. That small mistake on the ground floor is multiplied over and over again the higher you go. It is the reason Moses could not enter the Promised Land. He mistreated his role of favor and struck a rock out of anger instead of speaking to it as God directed. It is the reason Ananias and Sapphira died in Acts 5 after lying to the Holy Spirit. The presence of the glory of God was so pronounced in the Church at that time that any deceptive practice would have devastating results in what God was building.

Church history is filled with countless stories of people who experienced great things in God, but who did not follow through with the level of devotion to Him that their experience required. They died an untimely death. This is especially tragic in Solomon's case, as he introduced the worship of false gods to God's people in such a way that it took them many generations to recover from it:

> But King Solomon loved many foreign women, as well as the daughter of Pharaoh: women of the Moabites, Ammonites, Edomites, Sidonians, and Hittites—from the nations of whom the LORD had said to the children of Israel, "You shall not intermarry with them, nor they with you. Surely they will turn away your hearts after their gods." Solomon clung to these in love. And he had seven hundred wives, princesses, and three hundred concubines; and his wives turned away his heart. For it was so, when Solomon was old, that his wives turned his heart after other gods; and his heart was not loyal to the LORD his God, as was the heart of his father David. For Solomon went after Ashtoreth the goddess of the Sidonians, and after Milcom the abomination of the Ammonites. Solomon did evil in the sight of the LORD, and did not fully follow the LORD, as did his father David. Then Solomon built a high place for Chemosh the abomination of Moab, on the hill that is east of Jerusalem, and for Molech the abomination of the people of Ammon. And he did likewise for all his foreign wives, who burned incense and sacrificed to their gods.
>
> 1 Kings 11:1–8

I have seen so many lives ruined through what seemed like minor compromises. I cannot count the number of times I have watched a young lady marry a nice guy, but one who either is not a believer or does not have the same level of passion for God that she has. It does not take long before she becomes like him. The lower standard wins. (It happens to guys, too; just not as often in my experience.)

For Solomon, all this started with worshiping God on the high places. Eventually, it became worshiping false gods on the high places. One of the greatest tragedies in stories like this is that it is never the leader alone who falls. The bigger the leader's influence, the greater the number of people who become swept into his or her deception. Leadership is an honor and a privilege, but it is so costly when it is abused. When we are given much, we are judged by a much higher standard: "For everyone to whom much is given, from him much is required" (Luke 12:48). Solomon's wealth, fame, power and favor from God raised his required standards for life substantially. This is the high cost of blessing. The further we go in our journey with God, the less we can take with us.

Strength to Survive the Blessings

Here is the statement that breaks my heart the most in Solomon's story: "So the LORD became angry with Solomon, because his heart had turned from the LORD God of Israel, *who had appeared to him twice*" (1 Kings 11:9, emphasis added). God does not flaunt Himself. In fact, often He reveals Himself according to the measure of our hunger and our capacity to obey. When He appeared to Solomon twice, He put him in a category rarely experienced by anyone. In doing so, He qualified Solomon to become a great reformer and builder of thought, and also a developer of the revelation of God that was worked out in his city and nation's purpose for being. As great as Solomon was, so great was his collapse.

We have a serious problem here. Who among us does not want God to show up and bless us, grant us the fulfillment of our desires and give us clear direction for our lives? It is hard to imagine a person alive who would not want the kind of favor and blessing Solomon had. Yet God's heartbreak about Solomon must have been huge. This is one of the greatest betrayals ever. How many people in all of history can say that God appeared to them once, let alone twice? Very few indeed. And no one has ever been granted the favor and blessings that were given to Solomon.

So what about our becoming a blessed people, more blessed than we already are? What is God's intention? I am convinced that He disciplines us so that His blessings don't kill us. His desire to fill our lives with favor and blessing is far greater than all our desires for these things combined! But the question remains: Can we survive favor? Can we survive His blessings?

The apostle Paul gave us his insight on the matter in Philippians 4:12–13: "I know how to be abased, and I know how to abound. Everywhere and in all things I have learned both to be full and to be hungry, both to abound and to suffer need. I can do all things through Christ who strengthens me."

Paul's insight is this: The strength that we need when we are going through trial and facing lack is the same strength that we need when we are abounding in blessings. Blessings are never to replace our trust in God. But blessings that coexist with trust become the platform for the kind of increase that God alone can bring—it is the kind that has no sorrow attached (see Proverbs 10:22).

Developing a relationship with God that is unchanged in blessing or trial is one of the most important challenges we face as believers. We cannot go where we need to go in these last days without addressing these issues thoroughly.

12

A Theology of Blessing

We have some big challenges in front of us, and they may not be the ones you would first think of when we discuss the issues that challenge our faith. But it is true. Let me illustrate: We love it when people *seek first the kingdom of God*, but are not always happy with them when *all things are added* to them (see Matthew 6:33) We love it when people *humble themselves under the mighty hand of God*, but are not always as impressed with them when *God exalts them at the proper time* (see 1 Peter 5:6). We love it when we hear of those who have *given to God in secret*, but sometimes question their integrity when *God rewards them openly* (see Matthew 6:4).

We cannot go where God wants to take us if we cannot deal with God's process of bringing increase to His people. All increase has a purpose in the Kingdom, and it costs us dearly when we do not learn to value God's process or celebrate the one He is honoring. Jealousy often masquerades as discernment. It isn't. It is one of the most destructive forces in the Church—one that keeps us from real prosperity, which is in the soul.

The inability to celebrate another person's time of blessing and increase often disqualifies us from the measure that God had hoped to pour into our own lives. What we do with another person's possession (time of breakthrough) determines how and when we get our own (see Luke 16:12). Why would Jesus command us to rejoice with those who rejoice? The very fact that He commanded it implies that it does not come naturally to us since it is not our time of breakthrough. When rejoicing has to be commanded, it is because our circumstances don't lend themselves to joy. But believing the best about another person's time of increase and blessing is not only healthy for our soul; it also prepares us for increased responsibility and blessings in all areas of stewardship.

Significance

Discovering our significance in God's eyes is one of the most important and gratifying revelations we can ever receive. It frees us to live life as a joyful offering unto Him. But this is a frightening subject for those who are accustomed to maintaining "humility" by thinking of themselves with self-criticism and shame. Some religious leaders even resort to using humiliation to keep people in line, thinking it will make them more ready to obey the Lord. I doubt that many leaders ever think of this approach as abuse; they think of it as a necessary way to keep the people of God dependent on God. Once again, the end does not justify the means.

Learning our significance is vital. When Jesus revealed Himself to Saul on the road to Damascus, Saul saw the purpose for which he was chosen. He also saw what he would have to suffer in order to fulfill his purpose. I heard someone say once that vision gives pain a purpose. Certainly this was the case for this chosen one. Saul's significance was part of the revelation. It is vital to notice that it did not bring him pride or independence. Seeing significance correctly breeds trust and humility.

Our significance is tied directly to the One who has called us. It is not something based on our goodness; it is based on His. While it is true we that we are made in His image, it is also true that our righteousness is as filthy rags. Everyone is in need of a Savior who pays the ultimate price for us, that we might be called the righteousness of God. That is quite a change, made possible entirely by grace. Seeing our significance without increasing our trust in God always breeds entitlement. And entitlement leads us away from grace, a real cornerstone of our faith.

Everyone longs for significance. And it is Jesus alone who can give this thing that people long for—and that in abundance. It is costly, priceless and free.

How to Approach People

Years ago, I made a huge change in the way I approached and ministered to the people in the church I pastored. I used to come to them with the assumption that if they had their own way, they would sin. I saw myself as necessary to help keep them in a place of surrender and obedience to God. Through a series of events, it became apparent that I needed to change my approach and act as though I believed the people in my church were born again. That may sound funny at first, but think through it for a moment. If people are really born again, then they have a natural desire to obey God in all things. Their nature has been changed, and in their heart of hearts there is the passion and desire for God.

There is no question that born-again people still have the ability to sin. But what I learned was that what I gave attention to in people would grow. I decided to give attention to their God-given nature, speak to their heart of hearts and appeal to them as people who already had a desire to obey God.

The first thing this way of thinking did was change me. It is no fun being a self-appointed cop policing people's behavior—and more frightening, guarding people's intentions. (To be honest, this wrong way of leading did not dominate my life. But it would stick its ugly head up now and then, and it needed to be put to death once and for all.) Instead of trying to keep people from sin, I now faced the challenge of directing them toward their God-given destinies. The people responded to this change in me with a hunger to hear more, a hope for fulfillment in a God-centered future and a simple devotion to the Lord Jesus Christ. It is the very thing they had been waiting to hear, whether they realized it or not.

Jesus thinks differently about things than we do. He did not fear that His twelve disciples would be used beyond their maturity level in the ministry of power. Ministry would give opportunity for Kingdom power to touch people, and it would dial up things that needed addressing in the thoughts and values of the Twelve. When they responded with pride, superiority and murderous ideas, Jesus did not change His plans about when to release His followers in power (see Luke 9).

In fact, shortly afterward He chose and anointed seventy more disciples and imparted to them the same grace for the miracle lifestyle (see the beginning of Luke 10). Whatever people's shortcomings, He kept directing them toward their God-given destinies.

The Will of God

Many think that whatever happens in life is God's will. They say, "If it wasn't God's will, it wouldn't have happened." That way of thinking is devastating to God's purposes in the earth. It assumes that because God did not stop something from happening, it was His will—or at least He approved of it. That way of thinking, along with the language used to describe it, has infected more hearts with unbelief than anything else I can think of.

The Bible says God has no pleasure in the death of the ungodly and that He wants all to come to repentance (see Ezekiel 18:23, 32; 2 Peter 3:9). That is His will. Anything that happens differently has happened for a reason other than His will. The reality we live with is that the problems we face are often surrounded by many things that we do not yet know how to dismantle. To label something that is evil as coming from God is to credit God with evil. Instead, I keep what I call a *mystery file*. It is safer than attributing evil to God.

The error in logic people often make is that they misinterpret God's ability to turn whatever happens into something good as being a sign that a problem originally came from Him. For example, when persecution takes place, is it God's will? If it were, He would not have given us instructions about how to live a peace-filled life (see 1 Timothy 2:1–4). It is true that God has proven over and over again that He can turn opposition to the Gospel into a means of bringing about promotion for His movements and for persecuted individuals. We cannot mistakenly think, however, that this means the persecution was His will to begin with.

If sickness is God's will, why did He provide the prayer of faith for healing? Attributing everything that happens to God is a spiritually lazy way to think and live. He reveals His will so that we will know what to fight for. Why did Jesus raise people from the dead? Because not everyone died in God's timing. Jesus rebuked the storm because there was a spiritual power behind it that was not from the Father. The thought that God sent the storm so Jesus could rebuke it is silly at best. There is enough drama in life without our heavenly Father creating more of it just to keep us busy.

We were placed in the middle of a war, with an assignment to see the Kingdom come "on earth as it is in heaven." When Jesus said there would be wars and rumors of war, He was not giving us a promise. He was revealing the conditions into which He was sending His last days' army. I don't understand why so many believers can quote the verses that deal with God's judgment in the last days, but know nothing of the promises of blessing. It is an inconsistency that could cost us greatly. It is not that we should forget the hard stuff. It is that we need to remember some things that will help define our purpose.

Isaiah 60:1–2 (NASB) is a great example of this: "Arise, shine . . . darkness will cover the earth." The contrast is there. In the middle of the dark events is where we really find our place. And from there we are to have full effect on the nations.

Bad News/Good News

You have heard the bad news; here is the good: Jesus wins. In fact, Jesus already won. We don't fight for victory as much as we fight from the victory of Christ toward life. His victory was over every enemy of humanity—over sin, death, the grave and all the powers of darkness. His Gospel is the power of God unto salvation. His salvation touches every part of life, including the purposes of God for cities and nations.

My conviction is that often, we see from Scripture what our faith allows us to see. And because there is so little faith in the power of the Gospel to bring actual transformation during our lifetime, we tend to put the glorious promises of God off to the Millennium or consider them as descriptions of heaven. Yet these promises are in the Bible, with good reason for us to believe they are for now. As a result, they deserve more than a casual glance. Here are some prophetic words worth remembering when we think of the last days:

> Therefore they shall come and sing in the height of Zion, *streaming to the goodness of the* LORD—for wheat and new wine and oil, for the young of the flock and the herd; their souls shall be like a well-watered garden, and they shall sorrow no more at all.
>
> "Then shall the virgin rejoice in the dance, and the young men and the old, together; for I will turn their mourning to joy, will comfort them, and make them rejoice rather than sorrow. I will satiate the soul of the priests with abundance, and *My people shall be satisfied with My goodness*, says the LORD."
>
> Jeremiah 31:12–14, emphasis added

People will stream to God's goodness. They will also be *satisfied*, which means they will be filled to the brim, immersed in and totally satisfied by God's goodness. In this passage, the soul of the priest will also be overwhelmingly complete and fulfilled. Remember that every believer is a priest unto the Lord. To have the soul of the priest fully satisfied could very well be speaking of the prosperous soul the first verse of 3 John refers to: "Beloved, I pray that you may prosper in all things and be in health, just as your soul prospers." Ministry out of the abundance of the heart has always been God's intention for us all. Our internal reality was always meant to impact and define our external reality. This thought is clearly presented in John's epistle.

The fear of the Lord has become a very unpopular topic in recent days. People say it is a contradiction to our life under grace. While I understand their logic, I don't believe that kind of logic holds up against the evidence of Scripture:

> I will cleanse them from all their iniquity by which they have sinned against Me, and I will pardon all their iniquities by which they have sinned and by which they have transgressed against Me. Then it shall be to Me a name of joy, a praise, and an honor before all nations of the earth, who shall hear all the good that I do to them; *they shall fear and tremble for all the goodness and all the prosperity that I provide for it.*
>
> Jeremiah 33:8–9, emphasis added

The Bible must shape our logic, not the other way around. The fear of God is real and necessary. He is not only my Father, the lover of my soul and my comforter. He is almighty God.

The following passage from Hosea reveals the most important kind of fear: "Afterward the children of Israel shall return and seek the LORD their God and David their king.

They shall fear the LORD and His goodness in the latter days" (Hosea 3:5, emphasis added). It is the fear of God that comes from seeing His goodness. The psalmist also brings this to the forefront in Psalm 130:3–4, when he speaks of God's forgiveness: "If You, LORD, should mark iniquities, O LORD, who could stand? But there is forgiveness with You, that You may be feared."

I don't think there is healthy fear of God apart from seeing His goodness. And I don't think there is a true understanding of His goodness without fearing Him. The forgiveness that comes from His glorious goodness is our introduction to the fear of God.

I actually find the verse in Hosea shocking. When earthly blessings such as promotion at work, favor in the city or being well-loved by influential people come on the life of pre-believers, they may think they have earned them. But what measure of blessing would have to come for people to actually fear God because of it? I believe it would need to be extreme, but I also believe He gives us favor because of His love for those around us. And we are to pass that favor on to those who are observing His favor on our lives.

Who Is Israel?

I don't believe in replacement theology, where the Church takes the place of Israel in prophecy. That extreme is costly in numbing us to what really matters to God. The Israelites are His covenant people. But I also am deeply concerned that so many don't see the Church included at all in some of the prophecies that have Israel's name on them. For many, the Church seems to be a pause in the great unfolding of God's plans for His people, Israel, without any consideration for those who were grafted into that tree (see Romans 11:17–20). That, too, is an unhealthy extreme.

The Bible states that the Church is a holy nation and that the descendants of Abraham are children of promise, referring to the promise of salvation (see 1 Peter 2:9; Romans 9:6–8). While replacement theology is dangerous, I wonder how costly it has been that many do not see the Church mentioned in the prophets. This mistake robs us of a fuller understanding of our purpose and identity. *We won't spend what we don't know we have in the bank.* In other words, without a clear understanding of who we are in God's plan, we will not take the risks necessary to see His purposes fulfilled. This lack affects us in devastating ways. It robs us from thinking in a way that produces the transformation God intends.

Think about the Church in relation to this prophecy: "Now it shall come to pass *in the latter days* that the mountain of the LORD's house shall be established on the top of the mountains, and shall be exalted above the hills; and *all nations shall flow to it*" (Isaiah 2:2, emphasis added). Mountains are often used as a symbol of governments and powers. If that is the case here, then the house of the Lord (the Church) becomes the top of all other mountains or powers—not in dominance, but in influence. In this case, the mountain of the Lord's house refers to Mt. Zion, which is where the Tabernacle of David was pitched. It was not a high mountain, but all the other mountains were envious of Zion (see Psalm 68:16–18). This mountain had the Ark of the Covenant and the worshiping community of believers. That glory was missing from all the other high places. The result was that nations streamed to the Lord.

Both Mt. Zion and the Tabernacle of David are terms used to describe the New Testament Church, therefore causing this verse from Isaiah 2 to take on meaning for us right now (see Hebrews 12:22; Amos 9:11; Acts 15:16). At the same time, it reveals the power involved with authentic worship and how it clears the air of dark spiritual influence, enabling people to see clearly so that they might come to Christ (see Psalm 68:1–3). This is also seen elsewhere in Scripture. One great example is in Isaiah, where we see that people going through the *gates*, which refer to *praise*, are actually clearing the way for others (see Isaiah 60:18; 62:10).

The Isaiah 2:2 passage we looked at is repeated in Micah 4:1 because of its importance. Both times, it is earmarked with the phrase *last days*. It is inconsistent to believe the well-known Joel 2 passage about the outpouring of the Holy Spirit in the last days, but then reject the promises that pertain to victory and influence over nations.

Burning Hearts

My heart burns for the people of God to see the significance of the hour we live in and the equally significant call of God on our lives. I live conscious of the apparent paradox of Isaiah 60, with both light and darkness in the earth. (For what it is worth, there is not war between light and darkness. When a light is turned on, darkness leaves automatically. There is no fight. Light is that superior.) But I refuse to feed my heart with the bad news and call it being prophetically aware. I will only feed my heart with what God has done and what He is saying. I must be positioned to see the full impact of the Gospel of good news released wherever possible.

Recently, I have been speaking frequently from one particular chapter of the Bible in almost every city I travel to. While it is not the only message I bring, I always hope for the chance to speak on it at least once during every visit. It is Psalm 67. After I had been traveling around with this message burning in me, a friend called. He had not been to any of the places I had been, nor had he been in any of the meetings at home when I had talked on this chapter. Yet he told me that he thought Psalm 67 was to become a theme chapter for me.

I love it when God confirms the very things that burn in our hearts the most. It is that kind of message that we have the greatest responsibility to release in the earth. Psalm 67 says this:

> God be merciful to us and bless us,
> And cause His face to shine upon us. Selah.
> That Your way may be known on earth,
> Your salvation among all nations.
>
> Let the peoples praise You, O God;
> Let all the peoples praise You.
> Oh, let the nations be glad and sing for joy!
> For You shall judge the people righteously,
> And govern the nations on earth. Selah.
>
> Let the peoples praise You, O God;
> Let all the peoples praise You.
> Then the earth shall yield her increase;
> God, our own God, shall bless us.
> God shall bless us,
> And all the ends of the earth shall fear Him.

This just might be the most reformational psalm in the Bible. It reveals the effect of God's touch on our lives and the impact it has on the nations of the world. It is important for us to take a verse-by-verse look at this important prophetic message for us today.

Verses 1–2

The psalmist starts with the prayer for blessing and for the shining face of God (favor) upon his life: "God be merciful to us and bless us, and cause His face to shine upon us. Selah. That Your way may be known on earth, your salvation among all nations." In doing so, he makes a profound qualification that he does not want the blessing of God apart from the recognized presence of God upon him.

Some think it is more mature and spiritual not to pray for blessing. This is untrue. It is absolutely foolish and selfish not to pray for a life filled with blessing. And it is costly, too, as it removes the very thing that reveals to the nations who God is. Jesus' primary revelation to people was that God is our Father. When people do not see that we are blessed, we assume that they will instead know what God is like through our sermons—which they seldom take the time to hear.

The psalmist then states that through blessing, God's way would be known in the earth. His way is His nature. The great revelation that will be released in the last days is the revelation of His nature. People don't know what He is like—period. They just don't know. So besides our sermons, our lives need to carry the message of who He is. Carrying the blessings, the gifts of God on our lives, reveals the nature of the One who gave us the gifts in the first place. Blessings preach! They have a voice of their own.

The conclusion to these two verses stuns me—salvation to the nations. Is this not what we all say we long for? It is here that the Word of God tells us how. Contained in the DNA of the Lord's blessing on a person's life is the invitation to come to know the Source of the blessing and find salvation. Think of it—His kindness really does lead to repentance. We owe people an encounter with God; therefore, be full of the Spirit. We also owe them a view of the blessed life, so they can see the hand of a loving Father on our lives.

Verses 3–4

These next two verses of Psalm 67 are a summons to the people of the nations to become worshipers: "Let the peoples praise You, O God; let all the peoples praise You. Oh, let the nations be glad and sing for joy! For You shall judge the people righteously, and govern the nations on earth. Selah." There is nothing greater, for we always become like whatever we worship. We worship God because of His worth, but it becomes transformational in nature because of our exposure to His glory.

Verse 2 contains the possibility of salvation visiting the nations, and verses 3–4 show the nations ministering to God. This change is what brings joy to the nations, giving them justice at last. God is the Judge. His judgment is not to be feared. In fact, in this case His judgment is part of why they have such joy. Judgment is good because it always vindicates someone. When we belong to Him, the blood of Jesus covers us. The Father sees us in His perfect Son, Jesus Christ. Judgment is then aimed at whatever would try to wrongly influence us and challenge our place in Christ. It is aimed against the spiritual forces of wickedness. Hell was created as a place of eternal torment for the powers of darkness. This is a judgment we will all rejoice in. It is also good to notice that God's judgments will affect entire nations for the good.

Verses 5–6

Following the judgments of God that affect nations, in these next verses the people of God are once again found giving Him praise: "Let the peoples praise You, O God; let all the peoples praise You. Then the earth shall yield her increase; God, our own God, shall bless us." But this time there is something else that happens, something that has been waiting to happen our entire lives. The earth cooperates and yields increase to us.

The earth is not worn out and without resources, as the enemy would like us to believe. God has saved the best for last. Creation has been waiting for a generation to arise that could handle blessing well, and with it bring the nations to Him as His inheritance. To this generation the earth yields its increase. There is more reserved in the ground than has ever been taken out. We will come to this realization in the days ahead.

> For the earnest expectation of the creation eagerly waits for the revealing of the sons of God. For the creation was subjected to futility, not willingly, but because of Him who subjected it in hope; because the creation itself also will be delivered from the bondage of corruption into the glorious liberty of the children of God. For we know that the whole creation groans and labors with birth pangs together until now.
>
> Romans 8:19–22

Is it possible that this passage is describing what the earth is waiting for? I believe it is. There must be a generation that knows who they are, why they are here and what they are to do. This is royalty at its finest, for this knowledge is not a tool for building personal empires. It is a tool to draw the empires of man to God Himself. Over and over again, the Bible says this will happen. Why not in our lifetime?

Verse 7

Psalm 67 ends not with a prayer, or even a song of praise. It ends with a bold declaration of faith: "God shall bless us, and all the ends of the earth shall fear Him."

This is a confession of the transformation that takes place in which nations are saved, they rejoice in God's defense and vindication, and they watch as the Lord brings this blessing now into their lives. Even the earth cooperates with their assignment and responds to their identities.

Royalty Gives

There is one thing about Solomon's life that comes into play in this chapter on the theology of blessing. It is a simple phrase in which Scripture discusses his effect on the queen of Sheba: "Now King Solomon gave the queen of Sheba all she desired, whatever she asked, besides what Solomon had given her according to the royal generosity. So she turned and went to her own country, she and her servants" (1 Kings 10:13).

Royal generosity is something that I believe will be more and more important as we discover who we are, why we are here and what royalty looks like from God's perspective. Solomon did not give the queen anything because she was in need. Giving to meet needs is the easiest gift to give. Giving to support the work of ministry is also easy for those who see both the command of God and the results unto eternity.

But royal generosity is the rarest kind of giving, and in some ways the most important of all, because it comes out of honor, and it comes from a transformed life. This kind of giving comes because I recognize who the person is I am giving to. Thus, my gift is a gift of honor. And it comes out of knowing who I am.

This kind of giving changes a person from the inside out. History tells a well-known story about Alexander the Great. He was once passing by a beggar and gave him several gold coins. Someone noticed that he gave gold coins and asked him why, mentioning that copper coins would have met the beggar's need.

To this, Alexander responded in royal fashion, "Copper coins would suit the beggar's need, but gold coins suit Alexander's giving."

Once again, we are to *reign with the heart of a servant, and serve with the heart of a king.*

13

The Power of the Broken

Wisdom is transformational in nature, and it is something every person has a hunger for, whether the person realizes it or not. But we must address the nature of wisdom in order to serve those around us consistently with this virtue.

Wisdom often provides answers to problems both great and small. It is the one thing that satisfies the heart as well as the mind. By its nature it sees beyond the obvious and is able to provide solutions that go beyond the immediate need. Answers that provide immediate relief are not always answers that work for the long haul. Not so with wisdom. It is eternal. And while every believer is called to walk in wisdom and provide an example of how to reign in life and speak a message that settles issues, wisdom has a root system that most would reject at face value. That root system is the cross:

Where is the wise? Where is the scribe? Where *is* the disputer of this age? Has not God made foolish the wisdom of this world? For since, in the wisdom of God, the world through wisdom did not know God, it pleased God through the foolishness of the message preached to save those who believe. For Jews request a sign, and Greeks seek after wisdom; but we preach Christ crucified, to the Jews a stumbling block and to the Greeks foolishness, but to those who are called, both Jews and Greeks, Christ the power of God and the wisdom of God. Because the foolishness of God is wiser than men, and the weakness of God is stronger than men.

For you see your calling, brethren, that not many wise according to the flesh, not many mighty, not many noble, are called. But God has chosen the foolish things of the world to put to shame the wise, and God has chosen the weak things of the world to put to shame the things which are mighty; and the base things of the world and the things which are despised God has chosen, and the things which are not, to bring to nothing the things that are, that no flesh should glory in His presence. But of Him you are in Christ Jesus, who became for us wisdom from God—and righteousness and sanctification and redemption— that, as it is written, *"He who glories, let him glory in the Lord."*

1 Corinthians 1:20–31, emphasis added

The cross is the wisdom of God. Self-denial, dying, going low in humility, choosing others, becoming the servant of all—all these are expressions of wisdom. And while wisdom also provides answers for the sometimes complex issues in life, it is most likely to germinate in the heart of one who does the *cross walk*—one who genuinely follows Christ. God is looking for people who will love not the world, so that He can entrust the world to them (see 1 John 2:15).

While wisdom that begins with the cross is not what people are asking for, it is what they are looking for. People often think they need answers to satisfy their minds, when what they really need is something that will bring divine order to their whole being. They need purpose and examples to follow in order to fulfill their purpose. When we function in wisdom, we serve that end.

Those who want wisdom in order to be the know-it-all and a present-day savior of people with problems are not ready to function well in this gift. We experience reigning in life consistently to the same measure that we are willing to be reigned over by a lord, the Lord of all.

When wisdom grows from that root system called the cross, it is no longer obtained through human reasoning. God often puts us in over our heads to remove us from the reasoning that brings temporary answers and long-term disasters. When we are overwhelmed, it activates the hearing ear in us, that we might be connected to the answers found in the Kingdom of God.

Poor in Spirit

Both David and Solomon had this attitude that Jesus taught about in the Sermon on the Mount: "The poor in spirit are happy, for they will see God" (see Matthew 5:3). Being poor in spirit does not mean engaging in self-criticism, self-condemnation or shame. Those things are foolish. It is not found in the people who belittle themselves to appear humble. In fact, false humility will keep us from our destiny. But true humility will take us to it. I am always careful around people who constantly berate themselves, because at my expense they might fulfill the Scripture, "You shall love your neighbor as yourself" (Matthew 22:39). If they criticize themselves, they will probably criticize me.

This was David's motto: "LORD, my heart is not haughty, nor my eyes lofty. *Neither do I concern myself with great matters*, nor with things too profound for me" (Psalm 131:1, emphasis added). Here is the most powerful man on the planet telling us his approach to life. To me, this sounds like a man who knew where his power came from and had no misunderstanding about his own significance. This is brilliant. While our significance has importance, it is also a trap if we don't handle it well. Paul warned of this trap by telling us not to think more highly of ourselves than we ought (see Romans 12:3).

Solomon started out with true humility. He prayed brilliantly,

> Now, O LORD my God, You have made Your servant king instead of my father David, but *I am a little child; I do not know how to go out or come in.* And *Your servant is in the midst of* Your people whom You have chosen, *a great people,* too numerous to be numbered or counted.
>
> 1 Kings 3:7–8, emphasis added

He was overwhelmed by the size of the task he was assigned. Most of us pray better when God puts us in over our heads in our assignment. In fact, if we don't feel overwhelmed, we probably don't see what He has made possible through our lives. We pray better and hear better because we trust better when possibilities are beyond our reach. This is one of the most important reasons to have a vision that is not humanly possible. It is also why Jesus commanded His disciples to heal the sick instead of praying for the sick (see Matthew 10:8).

God has a habit of assigning impossible things to those who will listen. It is His invitation to greater trust.

Christmastime

I think the story of the wise men is one of the more intriguing stories in the Bible. We don't know how many there were; we just know of the three different types of gifts they brought the Christ child—gold, frankincense and myrrh. Some think these men were royalty. Others recognize them as the academics of the day. Regardless, they are called "wise men" for good reason. They illustrated wisdom, unusually so.

They traveled for probably two years simply to worship the One who was born King of the Jews. Wisdom leads to worship. This King was a baby, so they came to worship Someone who could do nothing for them. Later, when Jesus was healing the sick, raising the dead and delivering profound messages that brought the biggest crowds to silence, we can imagine people coming to worship Him. In fact, it happened. But the wise men's worship was the purest kind. It cost them, and they had no way to profit from it personally. Wisdom leads to giving. They worshiped with open hands. In other words, they brought gifts to God. He is still a covenant-making God who honors offerings. It is true that we cannot buy things from God, but it is equally true that we will never get all that is in our hearts without sacrifice and generosity.

Luke 16:11 says, "Therefore if you have not been faithful in the unrighteous mammon, who will commit to your trust the true riches?" This verse makes it clear that our use of money has an effect on the true wealth God releases into our lives. True wealth is the reward of good stewardship, but it is not more money. Rather, it is what we are all hungry for—the spiritual realities that Jesus gives us. Let me put it this way: Natural wealth can buy one thousand people a meal; true wealth can multiply one meal and feed a thousand.

After the wise men found the Christ child and worshiped Him, they were supposed to return home. God spoke to them in a dream about not returning by way of Herod, as that king had commanded them. They obeyed the dream. Wisdom always obeys God over man if there is a discrepancy between the two.

What Is God's Dream?

Well over ten years ago, I remember standing next to a wall in a church where an all-day prayer meeting was being held. I had just met a pastor named Mike, whom I had corresponded with by email. He pastored a great church in Utica, New York.

Mike leaned over to me and said, "Bill, God is looking for a city that would belong entirely to Him. And once He gets that one city, it will cause a domino effect across the nation."

My eyes lit up, and I responded that I believed my city, Redding, California, was that city. Mike said the same thing about believing for his city. Of course, it has never been a race, one city against another. It has always been a race against time.

Perhaps thirty minutes later, I was in a different part of the room, standing in the same row of seats as a woman I had known for a few years. She was a prophetess.

This woman walked over to me and said, "Bill, God is looking for a city that would belong entirely to Him. And once He gets that one city, it will cause a domino effect across the nation."

It was word for word what Mike had spoken to me half an hour earlier. My heart began to burn, knowing I had just had a glimpse of the heart of God.

These kinds of events are more than cute coincidences. They are more than encouraging words to keep us going in the midst of difficulties. These words are profound declarations of the heart of God, carrying an invitation to fulfill His heart's cry. I found it impossible to think the same way after that, and I had already been intent on seeing my city transformed.

Jesus' Confession of Faith

Before Jesus ever healed anyone, raised anyone from the dead or performed any of His other miracles, He announced these faith decrees. He boldly declared that the Spirit of God was upon Him for this purpose. It was His confession of faith:

> The Spirit of the Lord GOD is upon Me, because the LORD has anointed Me to preach good tidings to the poor; He has sent Me to heal the brokenhearted, to proclaim liberty to the captives, and the opening of the prison to those who are bound; to proclaim the acceptable year of the LORD, and the day of vengeance of our God; to comfort all who mourn, to console those who mourn in Zion, to give them beauty for ashes, the oil of joy for mourning, the garment of praise for the spirit of heaviness; that they may be called trees of righteousness, the planting of the LORD, that He may be glorified.
>
> Isaiah 61:1–3

In these few verses Jesus describes His ministry before it ever happened. In Luke's version, Jesus also states that He would open the eyes of the blind (see Luke 4:18). For the next three and a half years, Jesus fulfilled this mandate from the Father perfectly. He took those whom others had given up on and made them *trees of righteousness*—stable and deeply rooted in their Christlike nature. Captives were released—those imprisoned because of the sins of others. Prisoners were also released—those imprisoned because of their own sins. He came to announce the favorable year of the Lord—the Year of Jubilee. That was the year everyone in Jewish culture looked forward to if they were in debt. Everything was forgiven, and everyone had a clean start. Jesus truly healed the whole man—spirit, soul and body. And He announced it in Luke 4:18–19.

But there is a part that we often forget. It holds some of the secrets to rebuilding cities. Look at Isaiah 61:4 (emphasis added): "And *they shall rebuild* the old ruins, they shall raise up the former desolations, and they shall repair the *ruined cities*, the desolations of many generations."

To correctly understand the "who" Jesus is talking about in verse 4, we have to look again at verses 1–3. The "who" He is talking about in those verses are the poor, the brokenhearted, the captives, the prisoners, those who are in debt, those who need justice, those who are in mourning, those who have suffered great loss and those who are heavy in heart. So here is the key to rebuilding cities: *the broken*. The broken are the key to restoration. The broken build best because they are so grateful for their own restoration.

It is in God's heart to restore the broken so completely on every level that they become contributors to society in fresh and new ways. It is in His heart for them actually to become part of the team He has called to rebuild cities to their place of intended glory.

What a plan that God would use the rejected by society and anoint them to become a resource for His restorative purposes revealed over a city! The secrets are sealed in the heart of the broken. Our value for them is what releases them to their destinies. As we value the least, so God values full restoration of cities. The broken are the key.

The promise of God continues in Isaiah 61:5–7:

> Strangers shall stand and feed your flocks, and the sons of the foreigner shall be your plowmen and your vinedressers. But you shall be named the priests of the LORD, they shall call you the servants of our God. You shall eat the riches of the Gentiles, and in their glory you shall boast. Instead of your shame you shall have double honor, and instead of confusion they shall rejoice in their portion. Therefore in their land they shall possess double; everlasting joy shall be theirs.

How do we know this prophecy is for us, right now? First of all, Jesus quoted verses 1–3, bringing this word into the Church age. Second, verse 6 says we shall be called the priests of the Lord. That is highly significant because both Exodus 19:6 and this passage pointed to a future time when this would happen, saying "you shall be" priests. But in 1 Peter 2:9, it says "you are" a royal priesthood—the time is now! It is safe to assume that the season when all God's people—not just the tribe of Levi—would be referred to as priests of the Lord would be the time when He unfolds many of the promises that have been withheld until that perfect timing. I would like to suggest that right now is a perfect time for us to pray and ask God how much of these promises He will allow us to see in our lifetime. Praying for these promises as possibilities in our lifetime is the absolute minimum we must do.

These verses in Isaiah 61 add that we will experience prosperity and priestly ministry to God, while benefiting from the resources of those who refuse to follow Christ. All this is for the purpose of advancing the Kingdom. Double portion blessing and extreme joy will accompany the people of God in this season. Is this possible in our lifetime? I think so. It is worth bringing before the Father.

The anointing upon Jesus was an anointing of power. It was to heal broken people, who, in turn, would then heal broken cities. And now that same anointing and assignment is upon us because God loves cities and wants them to fully step into their place in the redemptive work of Christ on the earth.

14

Living Full

After sin entered the picture in Genesis 3, the Lord immediately set in motion the plan of redemption. Because those made in His image had turned from Him and obeyed the serpent, a man would need to become a perfect sacrifice. Jesus, God's Son, came as a Man, in man's image, to take our place in death. But the target of the Lord was not just for people to be born again, as glorious and necessary as that is. That was no doubt the immediate target, yet our conversion is also unto something. God's target for every person alive is to be *filled with the fullness of God*. I believe that is one of the incomprehensible thoughts in Scripture. But for us to qualify for God's ultimate target, we must first be born again.

That Christ may dwell in your hearts through faith; that you, being rooted and grounded in love, may be able to comprehend with all the saints what is the width and length and depth and height—to know the love of Christ which passes knowledge; *that you may be filled with all the fullness of God.*

Ephesians 3:17–19, emphasis added

When Jesus came to earth, He came to die in our place, making the payment for our sins. He both *redeemed* us and was *redemption's price.* After His death, He rose from the dead and appeared to the disciples, announcing that He now had all authority in heaven and on earth:

And Jesus came and spoke to them, saying, "All authority has been given to Me in heaven and on earth. Go therefore and make disciples of all the nations, baptizing them in the name of the Father and of the Son and of the Holy Spirit, teaching them to observe all things that I have commanded you; and lo, I am with you always, even to the end of the age."

Matthew 28:18–20

These verses are referred to as the Great Commission. Here His disciples were given all the authority they would need to accomplish His assignment for them. But in Luke's gospel, Jesus added one other thing that they would need: "Behold, I send the Promise of My Father upon you; but tarry in the city of Jerusalem until you are endued with *power from on high*" (Luke 24:49, emphasis added).

While Jesus was on the earth, the disciples operated in the power and authority He gave them (see Luke 9:2). But once He died, they needed their own commission and anointing. They could no longer draft off Jesus' personal assignment from the Father. In the Matthew 28 commission, they received authority. But now they would also need power. Authority came in the commission, to the degree that they yielded to their mission. Power came in the encounter. They were to stay in Jerusalem until they had the encounter God had designed and received the power He intended for them. It happened according to the promise given in Joel 2 that God would pour out His Spirit. Acts 2:4 tells us, "And they were all filled with the Holy Spirit and began to speak with other tongues, as the Spirit gave them utterance."

Being filled with the Spirit of God is perhaps the greatest privilege we can have in this life. It is evidence that the Father believes in the work He is doing in us enough to entrust the Holy Spirit to us, to dwell in us and rest upon us. And as great as this ongoing experience is in our lives, He has a purpose in giving us this privilege that goes beyond our personal blessings. In this encounter, He clothes us with power. Power is the purpose and evidence of a person being filled with God. Power is for miracles and endurance, both of which are designed to give witness to the resurrection of Christ.

The Multifaceted Gift of God

Truth is multidimensional, with layer after layer being built into our understanding and lifestyle. Truth is the multifaceted gift of God. As soon as we learn truth, He sets us up to learn it once again, this time from another angle. It is like the layers of an onion. He peels back layer after layer, exposing us to Kingdom realities we never knew existed. I have a sense this will continue for eternity. Paul spoke of it when he said that *"in the ages to come* He might show the exceeding riches of His grace in His kindness toward us in Christ Jesus" (Ephesians 2:7, emphasis added).

Truth sets us free—freer and freer, until it becomes cellular—a part of us. (It is time for the Word to become flesh again, in us.) A person is never freer than when yielding to the truths of God's Word. It is a beautiful dance of the human will surrendered to the purposes of God, where both God and His people share perfect delight. It is from this place of surrender that we live in fullness and purpose. As someone once said, freedom is not being able to do whatever we want; freedom is the ability to do what is right.

Being devoted to the absolute authority of God's Word is vital, regardless of the wisdom of the day. This world's wisdom is foolishness to God. In embracing the absolute truth of Scripture, we embrace the ultimate journey of growing in the knowledge of Him. Truth is absolute, but to increase in our understanding, we must recognize that "we know in part" (1 Corinthians 13:9). Most everything we know now will receive many midcourse adjustments throughout our lives, where God adds another facet to what He has already worked into us. This process is similar to the pruning Jesus talked about in John 15:1–3, where God prunes what is healthy and bearing fruit. It is not punishment. It is God's commitment to position us for continual increase. Truth has that effect, bringing much fruit in and through our lives for the glory of God.

I also compare this to the wineskin analogy that Jesus taught in Matthew 9:17. If wineskins are new, they will expand as the new wine expands. If they are old, they will tear and become ruined as the wine expands. As the Holy Spirit works deeper and deeper in our lives, our understanding of Him expands and increases. We must be firm in our devotion to the Word of God, but be elastic in the sense that we know God will increase our experience of Him with our increased revelation of Him. Those who become rigid break easily in a move of God that contains fresh revelation of His work and purposes in the earth.

This promise was given to the church at Ephesus: "That the God of our Lord Jesus Christ, the Father of glory, may give to you *the spirit of wisdom and revelation in the knowledge of Him*" (Ephesians 1:17, emphasis added). The Ephesians were the only ones who received a letter from Paul in which there was no correction of any kind. So what do you pray for the ones who have everything? That God would give them the spirit of wisdom and revelation in the knowledge of Him.

Fearing the Voice

In Exodus 20, Israel feared the voice of God because of all the supernatural events that surrounded it. Today it is different in that there are many who fear just the idea of receiving revelation from God. Their thought is that we will make our revelation equal to Scripture. The concern is legitimate, as some believers have made that mistake throughout history. And most of this group has had an intense love of Scripture, which is wonderful. But when we reject hearing the voice of God because we are trying to protect ourselves from the deception of making such revelation equal to Scripture, that is another deception altogether. Rejecting what God has to say out of the fear of abuse is no excuse. Even our faith rests in the fact that we heard Him call us unto salvation, and we responded. This was not in addition to Scripture, but instead confirmed it through the miracle of our own conversion.

Jesus only said what He heard His Father say. He is our model, which tells us that we can and must learn to do as He did. But Jesus went on to say, "The words that I speak to you are spirit, and they are life" (John 6:63). When He spoke,

His words became spirit, and the Spirit gave life through them. Hearing the voice of the Father was essential in order for Jesus to do what He did. And He called us to do the same, saying, "As the Father has sent Me, I also send you" (John 20:21). We must follow His example, not the example of those who model the fear of His manifested presence in the name of wisdom.

Line upon Line

When God reveals something new to us, He puts it in the context of what we have already learned, much like a jeweler putting a diamond in the setting on a ring. A previous truth often holds the new truth in its place. For example, when Jesus told His disciples that He no longer called them servants, but called them friends, that was a new concept entirely (see John 15:15). They had seen Jesus model the servanthood role brilliantly. They had seen Him as the ultimate example of a Son. He was the Son of God, who also referred to Himself as the Son of Man. But now they were being introduced to the concept of friendship with God. This truly was completely new.

It is helpful to acknowledge what the disciples had learned up to this point. They had learned that they were to lay down their lives to follow Jesus. They also had learned by His example what it meant to be a servant of all; Jesus had girded Himself with a towel to wash their feet (John 13:3–5). They had received instructions, rebukes, corrections and words of affirmation. They had succeeded as good servants. That became the context for this new revelation: They were friends—friends of God.

The concept of tender friendship with God, where we know what God is thinking and doing (as contrasted with servants who do not know what their master is doing), is put in the context of our experience as servants. This is important, because it would be erroneous to think that our friendship with God replaces our responsibility to serve. Friendship is held in the context of servanthood, just as a diamond is held in the setting of a ring. Serving God with all our strength and drawing near to Him in tender friendship are the most brilliant realities held in tension.

What Does Full Look Like?

The Old and New Testaments give us two completely different pictures of what it means to be full of the Holy Spirit. Is this a contradiction? Or is this the ultimate example of the diamond held in its God-designed setting, where two unusual definitions actually complement and complete one another? Obviously, I believe the latter.

The first mention of a subject in Scripture creates a definition of that subject that the rest of Scripture serves or adds to. That first mention is like a stake in the ground by which everything else is measured. The first mention of being filled with the Holy Spirit is one of the greatest examples of this principle. Handled correctly, it will equip us as a transformational generation.

Let's look at that first mention of being filled with the Holy Spirit in the Old Testament. When it was time for Moses to build the Tabernacle in the wilderness, he would need someone with unusual gifts—coming out of the *fullness* of God's presence:

Then the LORD spoke to Moses, saying: "See, I have called by name Bezalel the son of Uri, the son of Hur, of the tribe of Judah. And I have *filled him with the Spirit of God*, in *wisdom*, in understanding, in knowledge, and in all manner of workmanship, *to design artistic works*, to work in gold, in silver, in bronze, in cutting jewels for setting, in carving wood, and to work in all manner of workmanship."

Exodus 31:1–5, emphasis added

All the things this passage mentions as manifestations of being full of the Holy Spirit—understanding, knowledge and creative workmanship—are connected to the expression of wisdom throughout the book of Proverbs. Wisdom demonstrated in and through our lives is one of the greatest needs of the hour. Such wisdom, shown through us, expresses the nature of God in a way that satisfies the cry of people's hearts to know what the heavenly Father is like.

The New Testament talks about Jesus wanting to build His eternal dwelling place (see Matthew 16:18; Ephesians 2:19–22). And He wanted to build it with generations whose gifts would come out of the *fullness* of His presence upon them:

But you shall receive power when the Holy Spirit has come upon you; and you shall be witnesses to Me in Jerusalem, and in all Judea and Samaria, and to the end of the earth.

Acts 1:8, emphasis added

When the Day of Pentecost had fully come, they were all with one accord in one place. And suddenly there came a sound from heaven, as of a rushing mighty wind, and it filled the whole house where they were sitting. Then there appeared to them divided tongues, as of fire, and one sat upon each of them. *And they were all filled with the Holy Spirit* and began to speak with other tongues, as the Spirit gave them utterance.

Acts 2:1–4, emphasis added

This manifestation of God upon and through His people brought to earth what wisdom alone could not provide— solutions to the impossibilities of life. Jesus came to illustrate the Father, and every time He brought healing, deliverance or forgiveness, He made His nature known by performing His works (see John 10:37–38; 17:4).

Different Streams

My background emphasizes the power aspect of the Gospel. Even though I saw very little of it growing up as it pertains to miracles of healing, it was still there in our theology. We saw the greatest miracle of all—salvation—regularly, with many completely transformed lives. Thankfully, there were also some who modeled the miracle lifestyle well. Today, I am happy to say that miracles have become much closer to normal and expected. I am now looking for the *unusual miracles* level of anointing mentioned in Acts 19:11, "Now God worked unusual miracles by the hands of Paul. . . ."

The power aspect of the Gospel is not optional. Powerlessness is inexcusable for the person in whom the Spirit of resurrection dwells. But tragically, this stream of the Church that emphasizes power has placed little value on long-term ministry to cities and nations. Too often, this stream has embraced overt ministry at the expense of covert ministry.

Another stream of the Church emphasizes the wisdom aspect of the Holy Spirit. Believers serve brilliantly in various professions, providing wonderful examples of living moral lifestyles, while also demonstrating stability and long-term purpose etched into their family lines. The impact of this stream on cultural values is beautiful. God often uses believers with this emphasis to start various kinds of mercy ministries devoted to caring for people's basic needs. This is truly wonderful. But tragically, the fear of power or the fear of its misuse has rendered this group ineffective in fulfilling the Great Commission. At times, they have embraced covert ministry at the expense of overt ministry.

Neither of these streams has fully succeeded in what they have set out to do. It is time for cross-pollination through a full-on demonstration of the presence of God and the power of being filled with the Spirit. We can no longer afford for these two streams, represented by unique ideologies, to remain separate expressions of Christ.

The wisdom group must have power, or they will provide answers for the here and now, but with little or no connection to eternity. Neither will they have answers to the issues of torment caused by a real devil, who must be dealt with according to the example Jesus gave us. Our goal must not simply be to have a better life in the here and now. Our goal must include the transformation of society, a transformation that must touch people's hearts if it is complete and authentic.

But neither can we afford to have a group who can provide the miracles, but who have no long-term commitment to cities and nations. Such an expression of power becomes a flash in the pan that deals with present problems, but does little to establish the ways of God in a culture. It also does little to make the move of God this group so loves sustainable over multiple generations.

It is time for these two streams to come together and learn what it really means to be full of the Holy Spirit. My dream is to see these streams merge through a mighty outpouring of the Holy Spirit. But this time, it must be more than whatever our stream tells us is best. It must be a complete and full representation of what being full of the Holy Spirit looks like throughout Scripture.

I believe it is the heart of God for us to see people live with both wisdom and power. Understanding, knowledge and creative expressions must join with miracles, signs, wonders and the supernatural ability to endure opposition as evidence of being truly filled with the Holy Spirit. We must also see how power can affect the manifestation of wisdom, and how wisdom can affect the demonstration of power. This would provide the most undeniable demonstration of the heart and nature of God that the world has ever seen. It would bring restoration to institutions that have lost their way. And it would confront the works of the devil against the human body and mind. This time, it would not be manifested through a gifted person or a particular denomination or movement. Instead, it would be manifested through a yielded generation. This would be a dream come true, and would become the tool we need for fulfilling the impossible assignment to disciple nations.

This manifestation of wisdom that impacts the spirit realm reveals the eternal purpose of God in His Church:

> To the intent that now the manifold wisdom of God might be made known by the church to the principalities and powers in the heavenly places, according to the eternal purpose which He accomplished in Christ Jesus our Lord.
>
> Ephesians 3:10–11

This theme experiences the great crescendo in the following two passages, and is meant to give us hope beyond reason:

To know the love of Christ which passes knowledge; that you may be filled with all the fullness of God.

Ephesians 3:19

Now to Him who is able to do exceedingly abundantly above all that we ask or think, according to the power that works in us, to Him be glory in the church by Christ Jesus to all generations, forever and ever. Amen.

Ephesians 3:20–21

We can and must know the love of God in an *experience that is beyond comprehension*. The heart can take us where the mind is incapable of leading us. The end result is that our experience/relationship with God in this way opens us up to being *filled with His fullness*. This fullness contains both wisdom and power.

That final passage shows us God's devotion to working in and through us beyond the reach of our prayers *(abundantly above all we can ask)* and beyond the reach of our mind *(abundantly above all we can think)*. What God would like to do in and through us in our lifetime has never even been a passing dream. It is beyond our reach. But it is not beyond His.

Embracing such promises creates a supernatural hope that helps us become participants in the impossible—where nations become discipled according to His Great Commission.

The Ultimate Ring

In both the Old and New Testaments, humanity co-labors with God to demonstrate what He is like. This responsibility and privilege is only possible in the measure that we are filled with His fullness. The analogy of a diamond and its setting can provide us with the most wonderful example of what it means to be full of the Holy Spirit. The *power* (the diamond) revealed in the New Testament is held in the context of the *wisdom* (the setting) revealed in the Old Testament. When it comes to being filled with power and wisdom, it is not either/or. It is both/and.

If living the lifestyle of wisdom and power is done well, we illustrate the nature of God and His passion for people in a way that invites them to Him and draws them into a loving covenant with Him. In a very real sense, it is this *ultimate ring*—power displayed in the setting of wisdom—that represents God's heart and the covenant of God with man. When this is manifested properly in our lives, it becomes similar to an engagement ring, in that it invites people into the relationship with God that was promised back in Genesis and made available through Jesus Christ.

Whereas the heart's cry of all humanity is to know God, we have the privilege of making Him known through wisdom and power in a way in which *His kindness leads to repentance.* This is our mandate—to glorify Him through the wisdom and power that flows from a life of purity and love. This is what it means to "re-present" Jesus, and this is what it takes to see "on earth as it is in heaven" become a reality, creating eternal impact in the here and now. This is the power that changes the world.

About the Author

Bill Johnson and his wife, Beni, are the senior leaders of Bethel Church in Redding, California. Together they serve a growing number of churches that have partnered for revival. This apostolic network has crossed denominational lines in building relationships that enable church leaders to walk in both purity and power.

The present move of God has brought Bill into a deeper understanding of the phrase "on earth as it is in heaven." Heaven is the model for our life and ministry. Jesus lived this principle by doing only what He saw His Father doing. Bill believes that learning how to recognize the Holy Spirit's presence and follow His lead will enable us to do the works of Christ and destroy the works of the devil. He also believes that healing and deliverance must become common expressions of this Gospel of power once again.

Bill and the Bethel Church family have taken on this theme for life and ministry. They are seeing healings happen with regularity, and these works of God are not limited to revival meetings. The church is learning how to take this anointing to their schools, workplaces and neighborhoods with similar results. Bill teaches that we owe the world an encounter with God, and that a gospel without power is not the Gospel that Jesus preached.

Bill and Beni live in Redding and have three married children and nine grandchildren.

More from Bill and Eric Johnson

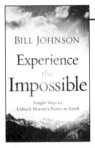

With wisdom and passion, Bill Johnson reveals how to access the power of heaven through the Holy Spirit. His simple, practical insights will transform not only the way you think, act and love but also the very atmosphere around you.

Experience the Impossible by Bill Johnson

Don't settle for a defeated, powerless existence. In this book, discover the significance of the mysterious truth: *Christ lives in you.* This means that the God of the universe trusts you—much more than you trust yourself! Find out how to move beyond the limitations you've placed on yourself and God, and start living with more passion, power and purpose.

Christ in You by Eric B. Johnson

✔Chosen

Stay up-to-date on your favorite books and authors with our free e-newsletters. Sign up today at chosenbooks.com.

f Find us on Facebook. facebook.com/chosenbooks

 Follow us on Twitter. @Chosen_Books

Key Books on Healing from Bill Johnson and Randy Clark

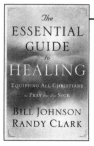

The ministry of healing is *not* reserved for a select few. In this practical, step-by-step guide, Bill Johnson and Randy Clark show how you, too, can become a powerful conduit of God's healing power.

The Essential Guide to Healing by Bill Johnson and Randy Clark

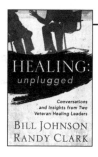

For the first time, Bill Johnson and Randy Clark candidly share their personal journeys behind life in the healing spotlight. With honesty, humor and humility, they recount the failures, breakthroughs and time-tested advice that propelled them into effective ministry.

Healing Unplugged by Bill Johnson and Randy Clark